Mmmm...
Casseroles

Mmmm... Casseroles

First published in 2010

LOVE FOOD is an imprint of Parragon Books Ltd

Parragon
Queen Street House
4 Queen Street
Bath BA1 1HE, UK

ISBN: 978-1-4075-9086-8

Printed in Indonesia

Design by Talking Design
Introduction by Linda Doeser

Notes for the Reader
This book uses imperial, metric, and US cup measurements. Follow the same units of
measurement throughout; do not mix imperial and metric. All spoon measurements are
level: teaspoons are assumed to be 5 ml, and tablespoons are assumed to be 15 ml.
Unless otherwise stated, milk is assumed to be whole, eggs and individual vegetables,
such as potatoes, are medium, and pepper is freshly ground black pepper.

The times given are an approximate guide only. Preparation times differ according to the
techniques used by different people and the cooking times may also vary from those
given as a result of the type of oven used. Optional ingredients, variations, or serving
suggestions have not been included in the calculations.

Recipes using raw or very lightly cooked eggs should be avoided by infants, the elderly,
pregnant women, convalescents, and anyone with a chronic condition. Pregnant and
breast-feeding women are advised to avoid eating peanuts and peanut products.
People with nut allergies should be aware that some of the prepared ingredients used in
the recipes in this book may contain nuts. Always check the packaging before use.

contents

introduction

There is nothing more comforting than a home-cooked casserole, whether tender beef and mushrooms immersed in a rich red wine sauce or a filling mixture of spicy vegetables and dried beans. While we tend to think of casseroles as cold-weather food, there are also many lighter dishes that are ideal for warmer times of year. What could be more delicious on a summer's evening than an aromatic fish and shellfish stew eaten alfresco or a colorful medley of Mediterranean vegetables served with fresh crusty bread.

The term casserole was originally applied just to the cooking utensil that we all recognize—an ovenproof pot with a lid—but soon came to refer to any dish cooked in it as well. Casseroling is a method of cooking that is slow and unhurried, allowing plenty of time for tougher cuts of meat and vegetables to become tender and for the cooking juices to thicken and acquire a rich flavor. However, the same could be said of stewing. The latter might involve using a little more liquid, although not invariably, and is traditionally cooked on the stove rather than in the oven.

There are many international versions of the casserole, with their variations in technique as well as ingredients. A French daube is a slowly braised dish that was once cooked in a tall casserole with a special lid that could be filled with hot charcoal. When suspended over the fire, it benefited from heat from below and above. A Moroccan tagine is a shallow, round earthenware dish with a conical lid that traps steam and so ensures that the ingredients are kept moist throughout the long cooking time over a small, round charcoal brazier. Like casserole, the word tagine is now applied to the dish as well as the vessel. Both dishes can be cooked just as successfully in a casserole in a modern oven.

Nowadays, the name casserole can be applied to a multitude of different dishes, but it is usually a one-pot dish with a mixture of ingredients—meat, poultry, fish, vegetables, and even rice or pasta—that is often served in the vessel in which it is cooked. It could be cooked in the traditional casserole dish, either on the stove or in the oven, in a pan, or even in a baking dish. It might be called a casserole, stew, ragout, cobbler, tagine, cassoulet, carbonade, or mole…the list goes on. Whatever it contains and however it's cooked, there is no denying that the casserole is a truly delicious dish!

top tips for success

- A flameproof, ovenproof casserole dish can be used to brown meat or other ingredients over direct heat on the stove before being transferred to the oven to finish cooking. Make sure to choose one with a tight-fitting lid to prevent moisture from being lost during cooking.

- When cutting up meat for a casserole, try to make the pieces the same size to guarantee even cooking. If some are much smaller than others, they may overcook and become stringy. Always remove and discard any gristle and trim off excess fat. Unless you are being particularly health conscious, you do not need to remove all marbled fat because it will add richness and flavor to the cooking juices. If you are worried about fat, the easiest way to be sure that almost all of it is removed is to prepare the casserole the day before it is required, chill it in the refrigerator, and then lift off any fat solidified on the surface before reheating.

- Meat is almost always browned first in order to seal in the juices and give it an attractive brown color. It may be coated in flour, which helps to thicken the cooking juices. Add the pieces of meat to the hot pan in small batches. Turn them over as soon as they are browned on one side, and remove with a slotted spoon when they are sealed all over.

- An easy way to coat pieces of meat with flour is to put them into a plastic bag, add the seasoned flour, hold the bag closed, and shake well. Shake off any excess flour from the meat before cooking.

- If the sediment in the bottom of the pan looks as if it might scorch, stir in a little of the recipe's liquid—water, wine, stock, beer, hard cider—between sealing batches of meat. Taste and, if it isn't burned, set aside to add with the main quantity of liquid later.

- Onions and sometimes other vegetables need to be softened before they are combined with the other ingredients. This is usually best done separately from browning the meat.

- Cooking times in the recipes are always guidelines rather than hard-and-fast rules and you cannot speed up the cooking without catastrophic results. Try to build a little "slack" into your schedule so that if your particular batch of meat or dried beans is not quite tender at the recommended time, the family won't faint from hunger when the casserole requires an additional 15–30 minutes in the oven. Do not increase the oven temperature in the vain hope that cooking will speed up.

- Check the quantity of liquid in the casserole from time to time during cooking. If it seems to be drying out, stir in a little hot stock or water. If the juices still seem to be a little too runny toward the end of the cooking time, remove the lid to allow the excess liquid to evaporate and the juices to thicken.

- For a fresh bouquet garni, tie 1 fresh thyme sprig, 2 fresh flat-leaf parsley sprigs, and 1 fresh bay leaf together with kitchen string. Use a long piece of string and tie to the handle of the casserole or pan so that the bouquet garni dangles into the hot liquid but is easy to remove. Do not forget to remove and discard the bouquet garni, or any other whole herbs or spices, such as bay leaves and cinnamon sticks, before serving.

béchamel sauce

makes about 2½ cups

- 2½ cups milk
- 1 bay leaf
- 6 black peppercorns
- slice of onion
- blade of mace
- 4 tbsp butter
- generous ⅓ cup all-purpose flour
- salt and pepper

1 Pour the milk into a pan and add the bay leaf, peppercorns, onion, and mace. Bring to just below the boiling point, then remove the pan from the heat, cover, and let steep for 10 minutes. Strain the milk into a pitcher and discard the flavorings.

2 Melt the butter in another pan. Add the flour and cook over low heat, stirring constantly, for 2 minutes. Remove the pan from the heat and gradually stir in the flavored milk.

3 Return the pan to low heat and bring to a boil, stirring constantly. Cook, stirring constantly, until thickened and smooth. Season to taste with salt and pepper.

beef stock

makes about 7½ cups
- 2 lb 4 oz/1 kg beef marrow bones, sawn into 3-inch/7.5-cm pieces
- 1 lb 7 oz/650 g braising beef in a single piece
- 12½ cups water
- 4 cloves
- 2 onions, halved
- 2 celery stalks, coarsely chopped
- 8 black peppercorns
- 1 bouquet garni

1 Place the bones in the bottom of a large pan and put the meat on top. Add the water and gradually bring to a boil, skimming off the foam that rises to the surface.

2 Press a clove into each onion half and add to the pan with the celery, peppercorns, and bouquet garni. Partially cover and simmer for 3 hours. Remove the meat and simmer for an additional hour.

3 Strain the stock into a bowl, let cool, cover, and store in the refrigerator. When cold, remove and discard the layer of fat from the surface. Use immediately or freeze in portions for up to 6 months.

chicken stock

makes about 11¼ cups
- 3 lb/1.3 kg chicken wings and necks
- 2 onions, cut into wedges
- 17½ cups water
- 2 carrots, coarsely chopped
- 2 celery stalks, coarsely chopped
- 10 fresh parsley sprigs
- 4 fresh thyme sprigs
- 2 bay leaves
- 10 black peppercorns

1 Place the chicken wings and necks and the onions in a large pan and cook over low heat, stirring frequently, until lightly browned.

2 Add the water and stir well to scrape off any sediment from the bottom of the pan. Gradually bring to a boil, skimming off the foam that rises to the surface. Add all the remaining ingredients, partially cover, and simmer for 3 hours.

3 Strain the stock into a bowl, let cool, cover, and store in the refrigerator. When cold, remove and discard the layer of fat from the surface. Use immediately or freeze in portions for up to 6 months.

fish stock

makes about 5⅔ cups
- 1 lb 7 oz/650 g white fish heads, bones, and trimmings, rinsed
- 1 onion, sliced
- 2 celery stalks, chopped
- 1 carrot, sliced
- 1 bay leaf
- 4 fresh parsley sprigs
- 4 black peppercorns
- ½ lemon, sliced
- 5⅔ cups water
- ½ cup dry white wine

1 Cut out and discard the gills from the fish heads, then place the heads, bones, and trimmings in a large pan.

2 Add all the remaining ingredients and gradually bring to a boil, skimming off the foam that rises to the surface. Partially cover and simmer for 25 minutes.

3 Strain the stock without pressing down on the contents of the strainer. Let cool, cover, and store in the refrigerator. Use immediately or freeze in portions for up to 3 months.

vegetable stock

makes about 8¾ cups
- 2 tbsp sunflower or corn oil
- scant ½ cup finely chopped onion
- scant ½ cup finely chopped leek
- ⅔ cup finely chopped carrot
- 4 celery stalks, finely chopped
- ¾ cup finely chopped fennel
- 1 small tomato, finely chopped
- 10 cups water
- 1 bouquet garni

1 Heat the oil in a large pan. Add the onion and leek and cook over low heat, stirring occasionally, for 5 minutes, until softened.

2 Add the remaining vegetables, cover, and cook for 10 minutes. Add the water and bouquet garni, bring to a boil, and simmer for 20 minutes.

3 Strain the stock into a bowl, let cool, cover, and store in the refrigerator. Use immediately or freeze in portions for up to 3 months.

Mmmm... meat

beef in red wine

serves 8

- 4 tbsp all-purpose flour
- 2 lb 4 oz/1 kg lean braising beef, diced
- 8 oz/225 g bacon lardons or diced bacon
- 4 tbsp olive oil
- 3 tbsp butter
- 16 pearl onions or shallots
- 3 garlic cloves, finely chopped
- 3¼ cups sliced mushrooms
- 2½ cups full-bodied red wine
- ¾ cup beef stock
- bouquet garni
- salt and pepper
- mashed potatoes, to serve
- fresh flat-leaf parsley sprigs, to garnish

1 Preheat the oven to 325°F/160°C.

2 Season the flour with salt and pepper to taste and toss the beef in it to coat. Shake off any excess.

3 Heat a large, flameproof casserole, add the lardons, and cook over medium heat, stirring frequently, for 5 minutes, until golden brown. Remove with a slotted spoon. Heat the oil in the casserole. Add the beef, in batches, and cook, stirring frequently, for 8–10 minutes, until browned all over. Remove with a slotted spoon.

4 Melt the butter in the casserole, then add the onions and garlic, and cook, stirring frequently, for 5 minutes, until light golden brown. Add the mushrooms and cook, stirring occasionally, for an additional 5 minutes.

5 Return the beef and lardons to the casserole, pour in the wine and stock, add the bouquet garni, and bring to a boil. Cover and transfer the casserole to the preheated oven. Cook, stirring 2–3 times, for 1¾–2 hours, until the beef is tender. Taste and adjust the seasoning, adding salt and pepper if needed. Remove and discard the bouquet garni. Serve immediately with mashed potatoes, garnished with parsley sprigs.

beef stew with herb dumplings

serves 6
- 3 tbsp olive oil
- 2 onions, finely sliced
- 2 garlic cloves, chopped
- 2 lb 4 oz/1 kg good-quality braising beef, trimmed and cut into strips
- 2 tbsp all-purpose flour
- 1 cup beef stock
- bouquet garni
- ½ cup red wine
- salt and pepper

herb dumplings
- scant 1 cup self-rising flour
- 4 tbsp lard or vegetable shortening
- 1 tsp mustard
- 1 tbsp chopped fresh parsley
- 1 tsp chopped fresh sage
- 4 tbsp cold water
- salt and pepper

1 Preheat the oven to 300°F/150°C.

2 Heat 1 tablespoon of the oil in a large skillet and fry the onions and garlic until soft and brown. Transfer to a plate.

3 Heat the remaining oil in the skillet. Add the beef, in batches, and cook, stirring frequently, for 8–10 minutes, until browned all over.

4 Sprinkle in the flour and stir well. Season well with salt and pepper. Pour in the stock, stirring all the time, then bring to a boil. Carefully turn the contents of the skillet into the casserole dish. Add the bouquet garni and wine. Cover and bake in the preheated oven for 2–2½ hours.

5 For the dumplings, place the flour, lard, mustard, parsley, and sage in a bowl with salt and pepper to taste. Mix well, then add enough of the water to form a firm but soft dough. Break the dough into 12 pieces and roll them into round dumplings.

6 Remove the casserole from the oven, discard the bouquet garni, and add the dumplings, pushing them down under the liquid. Cover, return to the oven, and bake for an additional 15 minutes, until the dumplings have doubled in size. Serve immediately.

beef goulash

serves 8

- 4 tbsp sunflower oil
- 2 lb 4 oz/1 kg braising beef, trimmed and cut into cubes
- 1 tbsp all-purpose flour
- 1 tbsp paprika, plus extra for sprinkling
- 2½ cups beef stock
- 4 tbsp butter
- 4 onions, chopped
- 2 carrots, diced
- 1½ tsp caraway seeds
- 1 tsp dried thyme
- 2 bay leaves
- 1 lb 12 oz/800 g canned chopped tomatoes
- 2 tbsp tomato paste
- 3 potatoes, diced
- salt and pepper
- sour cream, to serve

1 Preheat the oven to 325°F/160°C.

2 Heat the oil in a large skillet. Add the beef, in batches, and cook over medium heat, stirring frequently, for 8–10 minutes, until browned all over. Reduce the heat to low, sprinkle over the flour and paprika, and cook, stirring constantly, for 3–4 minutes. Gradually stir in the stock and bring to a boil, stirring constantly. Remove the skillet from the heat, pour the mixture into a casserole and rinse out the skillet.

3 Melt the butter in the skillet. Add the onions and carrots, and cook over low heat, stirring occasionally, for 5 minutes. Add the caraway seeds, thyme, bay leaves, tomatoes, and tomato paste, stir well, and cook for 5 minutes. Add the potatoes, season to taste with salt and pepper, and bring to a boil.

4 Remove the skillet from the heat and pour the mixture into the casserole. Stir, cover, transfer to the preheated oven, and cook for 1¾–2 hours, until the meat is tender. Taste and adjust the seasoning, adding salt and pepper if needed. Remove and discard the bay leaves. Serve the goulash immediately, topped with a swirl of sour cream and a sprinkling of paprika.

Mmmm...

vietnamese braised beef & carrots

serves 6

- ⅓ cup fish sauce
- ¼ cup granulated sugar
- 1 tsp five-spice powder
- 4 lb/1.8 kg beef short ribs or oxtail, or 3 lb/1.3 kg beef shin, cut into 2-inch/5-cm pieces
- 3 lemongrass stalks
- 1 tbsp vegetable oil
- 8 large garlic cloves, crushed
- 6 small-medium shallots, peeled
- 2-inch/5-cm piece fresh ginger, peeled and thinly sliced
- 5 cups coconut water (not coconut milk) or water
- 2–3 cups water
- 6 star anise
- 1 piece cassia bark or cinnamon stick, about 4 inches/10 cm long
- 4 fresh red Thai chiles or dried red Chinese (tien sien) chiles
- 4 large carrots, peeled and diagonally cut into ½ inch/1 cm thick pieces
- salt and pepper
- plain boiled rice, to serve

1 Put the fish sauce and sugar in a large bowl and whisk until the sugar is completely dissolved. Add the five-spice powder and mix well. Add the meat and turn to coat evenly. Transfer the marinade and meat to a sealable plastic bag and seal the bag, then let marinate in the refrigerator, flipping the bag over every hour or so, for 6 hours.

2 Meanwhile, discard the bruised leaves and root ends of the lemongrass, then halve and crush 6–8 inches/15–20 cm of the lower stalks.

3 Heat the oil in a large saucepan over high heat, then add the garlic, shallots, and ginger, and stir-fry for 5 minutes, or until golden. Add the coconut water, water, lemongrass, star anise, cassia, and chiles.

4 Reduce the heat to low–medium and add the meat and marinade with enough water to cover by about 1 inch/2.5 cm. Simmer, partially covered, for 2 hours, then add the carrots. Cook for an additional 2–3 hours, or until the meat is tender and falls off the bones. Adjust the seasoning with salt and pepper to taste.

5 Remove the fat from the surface of the casserole. Serve immediately with rice.

spicy beef cobbler

serves 4

- 2 tbsp all-purpose flour
- 2 lb/900 g braising beef, cut into bite-size chunks
- 2 tbsp chili oil or olive oil
- 1 large onion, sliced
- 1 garlic clove, crushed
- 1 small fresh red chile, seeded and chopped
- 1 zucchini, sliced
- 1 red bell pepper, seeded and cut into small chunks
- 1²⁄₃ cups sliced mushrooms
- 1 tbsp tomato paste
- 2 cups red wine
- 1 cup beef or vegetable stock
- 1 bay leaf
- salt and pepper

cobbler topping

- 1¼ cups self-rising flour, plus extra for dusting
- 2 tbsp baking powder
- pinch of cayenne pepper
- pinch of salt
- 3 tbsp butter
- 4–5 tbsp milk

1 Preheat the oven to 325°F/160°C.

2 Put the flour in a bowl and season well with salt and pepper. Add the beef, toss until well coated, and reserve any remaining seasoned flour. Heat half the oil in a large, flameproof casserole. Add the beef and cook, stirring, until browned all over. Remove with a slotted spoon. Heat the remaining oil in the casserole, add the onion, and garlic, and cook over medium heat, stirring, for 2 minutes, until softened. Add the chile, zucchini, bell pepper, and mushrooms and cook, stirring, for an additional 3 minutes.

3 Stir in the reserved seasoned flour and the tomato paste, then stir in the wine. Pour in the stock, add the bay leaf, then bring to a boil. Reduce the heat and cook over low heat, stirring, until thickened. Return the beef to the casserole, cover, and bake in the preheated oven for 45 minutes.

4 Meanwhile, to make the cobbler topping, sift the flour, baking powder, cayenne pepper, and salt into a mixing bowl. Rub in the butter until the mixture resembles fine breadcrumbs, then stir in enough of the milk to make a smooth dough. Transfer to a lightly floured surface, knead lightly, then roll out to a thickness of about ½ inch/1 cm. Cut out circles using a 2-inch/5-cm cookie cutter.

5 Remove the casserole from the oven and discard the bay leaf. Arrange the dough circles over the top, then return to the oven for an additional 30 minutes, or until the topping is golden brown.

beef stew with olives

serves 6

- 2 lb/900 g stewing beef, such as chuck or leg, trimmed and cut into 2-inch/5-cm chunks
- 2 tbsp olive oil
- 1 lb 12 oz/800 g canned chopped tomatoes
- 2½ cups sliced mushrooms
- strip of finely pared orange zest
- 2 oz/55 g Bayonne ham, cut into strips
- 12 black olives

marinade

- 1½ cups dry white wine
- 2 tbsp brandy
- 1 tbsp white wine vinegar
- 4 shallots, sliced
- 4 carrots, sliced
- 1 garlic clove, finely chopped
- 6 black peppercorns
- 4 fresh thyme sprigs
- 1 fresh rosemary sprig
- 2 fresh flat-leaf parsley sprigs, plus extra to garnish
- 1 bay leaf
- salt

1 Combine the marinade ingredients in a bowl. Add the beef, stirring to coat, then cover with plastic wrap and let marinate in the refrigerator for 8 hours, or overnight.

2 Preheat the oven to 300°F/150°C.

3 Drain the beef, reserving the marinade, and pat dry on paper towels. Heat the oil in a large, flameproof casserole. Add the beef, in batches, and cook over medium heat, stirring, for 3–4 minutes, or until browned.

4 Add the tomatoes, mushrooms, and orange zest. Strain the reserved marinade into the casserole. Bring to a boil, cover, and bake in the preheated oven for 2½ hours.

5 Remove the casserole from the oven, add the ham and olives, and return to the oven for an additional 30 minutes, or until the beef is tender. Discard the orange zest and serve immediately, garnished with parsley sprigs.

beef casserole with mashed potatoes

serves 2
- 2 tsp vegetable oil
- 8 oz/225 g extra-lean braising beef, cut into 8 pieces
- 10 small shallots
- 1 garlic clove, crushed
- 1 tomato, chopped
- scant 1½ cups thinly sliced mushrooms
- ⅔ cup red wine
- scant ½ cup chicken stock
- bouquet garni
- 1 tsp cornstarch
- salt and pepper

mashed potatoes
- 2 starchy potatoes, sliced
- 1½–2 tbsp warm milk
- 1 tsp Dijon mustard

1 Preheat the oven to 350°F/180°C.

2 Heat the oil in a flameproof casserole. Add the meat and shallots and cook over high heat, stirring, for 4–5 minutes, until the meat is browned on all sides. Add the garlic, tomato, mushrooms, wine, stock, and bouquet garni. Bring to a simmer, cover, and transfer the casserole to the preheated oven for 45–60 minutes, or until everything is tender.

3 Meanwhile, place the potatoes in a saucepan of boiling water and simmer for 20 minutes, or until just tender. Remove from heat, drain well, and return to the saucepan. Add the milk and mash well. Stir in the mustard and keep warm.

4 Use a slotted spoon to remove the meat and vegetables from the casserole and transfer to a warmed serving dish. Cook the sauce on the stove over high heat until reduced by half. Reduce the heat, remove the bouquet garni, and adjust the seasoning, adding salt and pepper if needed.

5 Mix the cornstarch to a paste with a little cold water. Add to the sauce, stirring well, and bring back to a simmer. Pour the sauce over the meat and vegetables and serve immediately with the mashed potatoes.

meatball casserole

serves 4
- 2 tbsp olive oil
- 2 onions, chopped
- 2 garlic cloves, finely chopped
- 1 lb 2 oz/500 g carrots, cut into pieces
- 1 lb 2 oz/500 g potatoes, cut into pieces
- 1¼ cups beef stock or water
- 1 tbsp sweet paprika
- 2¼ cups strained tomatoes
- salt and pepper

meatballs
- 1 slice of bread, crusts removed, torn into pieces
- 1½ tbsp milk
- 10½ oz/300 g ground beef
- 2 tbsp chopped fresh parsley, plus extra to garnish
- 1 small egg
- salt and pepper

1 For the meatballs, put the bread into a bowl with the milk and let soak for 5 minutes. Put the ground beef, parsley, and egg into a separate bowl. Squeeze out the bread and add it to the bowl, then season to taste with salt and pepper. Mix well until thoroughly combined. Shape the mixture into 16 small balls. Put them onto a plate, cover, and let chill in the refrigerator for 30 minutes.

2 Heat the oil in a large pan. Add the meatballs, in batches if necessary, and cook over medium heat, stirring and turning frequently, until browned all over. Using a slotted spoon, remove from the pan and set aside.

3 Add the onions and garlic to the pan and cook over low heat, stirring occasionally, for 5 minutes. Add the carrots and potatoes, return the meatballs to the pan, pour in the stock, and bring to a boil. Reduce the heat, cover, and simmer for 15 minutes.

4 Sprinkle in the paprika and stir in the strained tomatoes. Re-cover the pan and simmer for an additional 15–20 minutes. Season to taste with salt and pepper, garnish with parsley, and serve immediately.

beef & pepper stew

serves 4

- 1 lb/450 g braising beef
- 1½ tbsp all-purpose flour
- 2 tbsp olive oil
- 1 red onion, chopped
- 3–4 garlic cloves, crushed
- 1 fresh green chile, seeded and chopped
- 3 celery stalks, sliced
- 4 whole cloves
- 1 tsp ground allspice
- 1–2 tsp hot pepper sauce, or to taste
- 2½ cups beef stock
- 8 oz/225 g squash, such as acorn, seeded, peeled, and cut into small chunks
- 1 large red bell pepper, seeded and chopped
- 4 tomatoes, coarsely chopped
- ¾ cup okra, trimmed and halved
- cooked rice, to serve

1 Trim any fat or gristle from the beef and cut into 1-inch/2.5-cm chunks. Toss the beef in the flour until well coated and reserve any remaining flour.

2 Heat the oil in a large, heavy-bottom pan and cook the onion, garlic, chile, and celery with the cloves and allspice, stirring frequently, for 5 minutes, or until softened. Add the beef and cook over high heat, stirring frequently, for 3 minutes, or until browned on all sides. Sprinkle in the reserved flour and cook, stirring constantly, for 2 minutes, then remove from the heat.

3 Add the hot pepper sauce and gradually stir in the stock, then return to the heat and bring to a boil, stirring. Reduce the heat, then cover and let simmer, stirring occasionally, for 1½ hours.

4 Add the squash and bell pepper to the pan and simmer for an additional 15 minutes. Add the tomatoes and okra, and simmer for an additional 15 minutes, or until the beef is tender. Serve immediately with rice.

beef enchiladas

serves 4

- 2 tbsp olive oil, plus extra for oiling
- 2 large onions, thinly sliced
- 1 lb 4 oz/550 g lean beef, cut into bite-size pieces
- 1 tbsp ground cumin
- 1–2 tsp cayenne pepper, or to taste
- 1 tsp paprika
- 8 soft corn tortillas, warmed
- 1 cup grated cheddar cheese
- salt and pepper

taco sauce

- 1 tbsp olive oil
- 1 onion, finely chopped
- 1 green bell pepper, seeded and diced
- 1–2 fresh green chiles, seeded and finely chopped
- 3 garlic cloves, crushed
- 1 tsp ground cumin
- 1 tsp ground coriander
- 1 tsp light brown sugar
- 1 lb/450 g ripe tomatoes, peeled and coarsely chopped
- juice of ½ lemon
- salt and pepper

1 Preheat the oven to 350°F/180°C. Oil a large, rectangular baking dish.

2 To make the sauce, heat the oil in a large skillet over medium heat. Add the onion and cook for 5 minutes, or until softened. Stir in the bell pepper and chile, and cook for 5 minutes. Add the garlic, cumin, coriander, and sugar and cook for an additional 2 minutes, stirring. Stir in the tomatoes and lemon juice, with salt and pepper to taste. Bring to a boil, then reduce the heat, and simmer for 15 minutes.

3 Heat the oil in a large skillet over low heat. Add the onions and cook for 10 minutes, or until soft and golden. Remove with a slotted spoon and set aside.

4 Increase the heat to high, add the beef, and cook, stirring, for 2–3 minutes, or until browned on all sides. Reduce the heat to medium, add the spices and salt and pepper to taste, and cook, stirring constantly, for 2 minutes.

5 Divide the beef mixture among the tortillas, top with three-quarters of the cheese, and roll up. Place the tortillas, seam side down, in the prepared dish, top with the taco sauce and the remaining cheese, and bake in the preheated oven for 30 minutes, until the topping is golden and bubbling. Serve immediately.

lasagna al forno

serves 4
- 2 tbsp olive oil
- 2 oz/55 g pancetta, chopped
- 1 onion, chopped
- 1 garlic clove, finely chopped
- 8 oz/225 g ground beef
- 2 celery stalks, chopped
- 2 carrots, chopped
- pinch of sugar
- ½ tsp dried oregano
- 14 oz/400 g canned chopped tomatoes
- 2 tsp Dijon mustard
- 1¼ cups grated cheddar cheese
- 1¼ cups hot Béchamel Sauce (see page 9)
- 8 oz/225 g dried no-precook lasagna sheets
- 1 cup freshly grated Parmesan cheese
- salt and pepper

1 Preheat the oven to 375°F/190°C.

2 Heat the oil in a large, heavy-bottom pan. Add the pancetta and cook over medium heat, stirring occasionally, for 3 minutes, or until the fat starts to run. Add the onion and garlic and cook, stirring occasionally, for 5 minutes, or until softened.

3 Add the beef and cook, breaking it up with a wooden spoon, until browned all over. Stir in the celery and carrots, and cook for 5 minutes. Season to taste with salt and pepper. Add the sugar, oregano, and tomatoes and their can juices. Bring to a boil, reduce the heat, and simmer for 30 minutes.

4 Meanwhile, to make the cheese sauce, stir the mustard and cheddar cheese into the Béchamel Sauce.

5 In a large, rectangular ovenproof dish, make alternate layers of meat sauce, lasagna sheets, and most of the Parmesan cheese. Pour the cheese sauce over the layers, covering them completely, and sprinkle with the remaining Parmesan cheese. Bake in the preheated oven for 30 minutes, or until golden brown and bubbling. Serve immediately.

lamb casserole with artichokes & olives

serves 4

- 4 tbsp strained plain yogurt
- grated rind of 1 lemon
- 2 garlic cloves, crushed
- 3 tbsp olive oil
- 1 tsp ground cumin
- 1 lb 10 oz/700 g lean boneless lamb, cubed
- 1 onion, thinly sliced
- ⅔ cup dry white wine
- 1 lb/450 g tomatoes, coarsely chopped
- 1 tbsp tomato paste
- pinch of sugar
- 2 tbsp chopped fresh oregano or 1 tsp dried
- 2 bay leaves
- ½ cup kalamata olives
- 14 oz/400 g canned artichoke hearts, drained and halved
- salt and pepper

1 Put the yogurt, lemon rind, garlic, 1 tablespoon of the oil, the cumin, and salt and pepper to taste in a large bowl and mix together. Add the lamb and toss together until coated in the mixture. Cover and let marinate for at least 1 hour.

2 Heat 1 tablespoon of the remaining oil in a large, flameproof casserole. Add the lamb, in batches, and fry for about 5 minutes, stirring frequently, until browned on all sides. Using a slotted spoon, remove the meat from the casserole. Add the remaining tablespoon of oil to the casserole with the onion and fry for 5 minutes, until softened.

3 Pour the wine into the casserole, stirring in any glazed sediment from the bottom, and bring to a boil. Reduce the heat and return the meat to the casserole, then stir in the tomatoes, tomato paste, sugar, oregano, and bay leaves.

4 Cover the casserole and simmer for about 1½ hours, until the lamb is tender. Stir in the olives and artichokes and simmer for an additional 10 minutes. Remove the bay leaves and serve immediately.

lamb stew with sweet bell peppers

serves 4

- 1 lb/450 g lean, boneless lamb, such as leg of lamb or fillet
- 1½ tbsp all-purpose flour
- 1 tsp ground cloves
- 1–1½ tbsp olive oil
- 1 white onion, sliced
- 2–3 garlic cloves, sliced
- 1¼ cups orange juice
- ⅔ cup lamb or chicken stock
- 1 cinnamon stick, bruised
- 2 red bell peppers (sweet pointed variety, if available), seeded and sliced into rings
- 4 tomatoes
- a few fresh cilantro sprigs, plus 1 tbsp chopped to garnish
- salt and pepper

1 Preheat the oven to 375°F/190°C.

2 Trim any fat or gristle from the lamb and cut into thin strips. Mix the flour and cloves together. Toss the lamb in the spiced flour until well coated and reserve any remaining spiced flour.

3 Heat 1 tablespoon of the oil in a heavy-bottom skillet and cook the lamb over high heat, stirring frequently, for 3 minutes, or until browned on all sides. Using a slotted spoon, transfer to a casserole.

4 Add the onion and garlic to the skillet and cook over medium heat, stirring frequently, for 3 minutes, adding the extra oil if necessary. Sprinkle in the reserved spiced flour and cook, stirring constantly, for 2 minutes, then remove from the heat. Gradually stir in the orange juice and stock, then return to the heat and bring to a boil, stirring.

5 Pour over the lamb in the casserole, then add the cinnamon stick, bell peppers, tomatoes, and cilantro sprigs and stir well. Cover and cook in the preheated oven for 1½ hours, or until the lamb is tender.

6 Discard the cinnamon stick and adjust the seasoning, adding salt and pepper if needed. Serve immediately, garnished with the chopped cilantro.

lamb shanks with gremolata

serves 4

- 4 trimmed lamb shanks
- 2 tbsp olive oil
- 4 garlic cloves, halved
- 1 dried chile, crushed
- 3 fresh rosemary sprigs
- 6 ripe plum tomatoes
- 2 large onions, finely chopped
- 4 strips of orange zest
- 2 bay leaves
- 1 tsp brown sugar
- generous ⅓ cup red wine
- 2¼ cups water
- salt and pepper

gremolata

- ¾ cup blanched, skinless almonds
- 2 garlic cloves, finely chopped
- grated rind of 2 lemons
- small bunch of fresh flat-leaf parsley, chopped

1 Preheat the oven to 350°F/180°C. Season the lamb well with salt and pepper. Heat half the oil in a flameproof casserole. Add the lamb to the casserole and brown for 3 minutes on all sides, then remove from the heat. Chop the garlic, chile, and rosemary and mix together.

2 Cut the tomatoes in half and, with the skin side in your hand, grate the flesh to form a rough tomato pulp. The skin will be left in your hand.

3 Remove the meat from the casserole and return the casserole to the heat with the remaining oil. Add the garlic, chile, and rosemary and fry for 2 minutes, until fragrant and aromatic. Add the onions and cook for about 5 minutes, until soft. Season to taste with salt and pepper.

4 Return the meat to the casserole with the orange zest, bay leaves, sugar, tomato pulp, wine, and water. Cover and let simmer, then transfer to the preheated oven and cook for 2½ hours, basting regularly.

5 Meanwhile, roast the almonds in the oven until golden brown. Let cool. When ready to serve, roughly chop the almonds and place in a bowl with the garlic, lemon rind, and parsley. Mix well. Transfer the lamb shanks to serving plates and scatter over a little of the gremolata. Serve immediately.

turkish lamb casserole

serves 4

- 2 tbsp olive oil
- 4 lamb shanks,
  about 10½ oz/300 g each
- 2 onions, sliced
- 2 bell peppers, any color,
  seeded and chopped
- 2 garlic cloves, crushed
- 1 eggplant, cut into small
  cubes
- ½ tsp paprika
- ½ tsp ground cinnamon
- 1¼ cups cooked chickpeas
- 14 oz/400 g canned
  chopped tomatoes
- 2 tsp mixed dried
  Mediterranean herbs
- scant ½ cup lamb or
  vegetable stock, plus extra
  if needed
- salt and pepper
- cooked couscous, to serve

1 Preheat the oven to 325°F/160°C.

2 Heat half the oil in a large, nonstick skillet over high heat, then add the lamb shanks and cook, turning frequently, for 2–3 minutes, or until browned all over. Transfer to a casserole.

3 Heat the remaining oil in the skillet over medium–high heat, then add the onions and bell peppers and cook, stirring frequently, for 10–15 minutes, or until the onions are softened and just turning golden. Add the garlic, eggplant, and spices, and cook, stirring constantly, for 1 minute. Add the chickpeas, tomatoes, herbs, and stock, stir well, and bring to a simmer. Season to taste with salt and pepper and transfer to a casserole.

4 Cover the casserole, then transfer to the preheated oven and cook for 1½ hours. Check after 45 minutes that the casserole is gently bubbling and that there is enough liquid—if it looks dry, add a little more stock or boiling water and stir in. Serve immediately with couscous.

mediterranean lamb casserole

serves 4

- pinch of saffron threads
- 2 tbsp boiling water
- 1 lb/450 g lean boneless lamb, such as leg steaks
- 1½ tbsp all-purpose flour
- 1 tsp ground coriander
- ½ tsp ground cumin
- ½ tsp ground allspice
- 1 tbsp olive oil
- 1 onion, chopped
- 2–3 garlic cloves, chopped
- scant 2 cups lamb or chicken stock
- 1 cinnamon stick, bruised
- ½ cup coarsely chopped dried apricots
- 1½ cups sliced zucchini
- ¾ cup cherry tomatoes
- 1 tbsp chopped fresh cilantro
- salt and pepper
- 2 tbsp coarsely chopped pistachios, to garnish
- cooked couscous, to serve

1 Put the saffron threads in a heatproof pitcher with the water and let stand for at least 10 minutes to infuse.

2 Trim off any fat or gristle from the lamb and cut into 1-inch/2.5-cm chunks. Mix the flour and spices together, then toss the lamb in the spiced flour until well coated and reserve any remaining spiced flour.

3 Heat the oil in a large, heavy-bottom pan and cook the onion and garlic, stirring frequently, for 5 minutes, or until softened. Add the lamb and cook over high heat, stirring frequently, for 3 minutes, or until browned on all sides. Sprinkle in the reserved spiced flour and cook, stirring constantly, for 2 minutes, then remove from the heat.

4 Gradually stir in the stock and the saffron and its soaking liquid, then return to the heat and bring to a boil, stirring. Add the cinnamon stick and apricots. Reduce the heat, then cover and simmer, stirring occasionally, for 1 hour.

5 Add the zucchini and tomatoes and cook for an additional 15 minutes. Discard the cinnamon stick. Stir in the cilantro and season to taste with salt and pepper. Serve immediately, sprinkled with the pistachios and accompanied by couscous.

tagine of lamb

serves 4

- 1 tbsp sunflower or corn oil
- 1 onion, chopped
- 12 oz/350 g boneless lamb, trimmed of all visible fat and cut into 1-inch/2.5-cm cubes
- 1 garlic clove, finely chopped
- 2½ cups vegetable stock
- juice and grated rind of 1 orange
- 1 tsp honey
- 1 cinnamon stick
- ½-inch/1-cm piece fresh ginger, finely chopped
- 1 eggplant
- 4 tomatoes, peeled and chopped
- ⅔ cup plumped dried apricots
- 2 tbsp chopped fresh cilantro
- salt and pepper
- cooked couscous, to serve

1 Heat the oil in a large, heavy-bottom skillet over medium heat. Add the onion and lamb and cook, stirring frequently, for 5 minutes, or until the meat is lightly browned all over.

2 Add the garlic, stock, orange juice and rind, honey, cinnamon stick, and ginger. Bring to a boil, then reduce the heat, cover, and simmer for 45 minutes.

3 Using a sharp knife, halve the eggplant lengthwise and slice thinly. Add to the skillet with the chopped tomatoes and apricots. Cover and cook for an additional 45 minutes, or until the lamb is tender.

4 Stir in the cilantro and season to taste with salt and pepper. Serve immediately with couscous.

french country casserole

serves 6

- 2 tbsp corn oil
- 4 lb 8 oz/2 kg boneless leg of lamb, cut into 1-inch/2.5-cm cubes
- 6 leeks, sliced
- 1 tbsp all-purpose flour
- ⅔ cup rosé wine
- 1¼ cups chicken stock
- 1 tbsp tomato paste
- 1 tbsp sugar
- 2 tbsp chopped fresh mint, plus extra sprigs to garnish
- ½ cup chopped, plumped dried apricots
- 2 lb 4 oz/1 kg potatoes, sliced
- 3 tbsp melted unsalted butter
- salt and pepper

1 Preheat the oven to 350°F/180°C.

2 Heat the oil in a large, flameproof casserole. Add the lamb in batches and cook over medium heat, stirring, for 5–8 minutes, or until browned. Transfer to a plate.

3 Add the leeks to the casserole and cook, stirring occasionally, for 5 minutes, or until softened. Sprinkle in the flour and cook, stirring, for 1 minute. Pour in the wine and stock and bring to a boil, stirring. Stir in the tomato paste, sugar, chopped mint, and apricots. Season to taste with salt and pepper.

4 Return the lamb to the casserole and stir. Arrange the potato slices on top and brush with the melted butter. Cover and bake in the preheated oven for 1½ hours.

5 Increase the oven temperature to 400°F/200°C, uncover the casserole, and bake for an additional 30 minutes, or until the potato topping is golden brown. Serve immediately, garnished with mint sprigs.

lamb stew with chickpeas

serves 6

- 6 tbsp olive oil
- 8 oz/225 g spicy sausage, cut into ¼-inch/5-mm thick slices, casings removed
- 2 large onions, chopped
- 6 large garlic cloves, crushed
- 2 lb/900 g boned leg of lamb, cut into 2-inch/5-cm chunks
- scant 1¼ cups lamb stock or water
- ½ cup red wine, such as Rioja or Tempranillo
- 2 tbsp sherry vinegar
- 1 lb 12 oz/800 g canned chopped tomatoes
- 4 fresh thyme sprigs, plus extra to garnish
- 2 bay leaves
- ½ tsp sweet paprika
- 1 lb 12 oz/800 g canned chickpeas, rinsed and drained
- salt and pepper

1 Preheat the oven to 325°F/160°C.

2 Heat 4 tablespoons of the oil in a large, flameproof casserole over medium–high heat. Reduce the heat, add the spicy sausage, and cook for 1 minute. Transfer to a plate. Add the onions to the casserole and cook for 2 minutes, then add the garlic and continue cooking for 3 minutes, or until the onions are soft but not brown. Remove from the casserole and set aside.

3 Heat the remaining oil in the casserole. Add the lamb, in batches if necessary, and cook until browned all over.

4 Return the onion mixture and spicy sausage to the casserole. Stir in the stock, wine, vinegar, tomatoes, and salt and pepper to taste. Bring to a boil, scraping any glazed sediment from the bottom of the casserole. Reduce the heat and stir in the thyme, bay leaves, and paprika.

5 Transfer to the preheated oven and cook, covered, for 40–45 minutes, until the lamb is tender. Stir in the chickpeas and return to the oven, uncovered, for 10 minutes.

6 Taste and adjust the seasoning, adding salt and pepper if needed. Serve immediately, garnished with thyme sprigs.

pasticcio

serves 4

- 1 tbsp olive oil
- 1 onion, chopped
- 2 garlic cloves, finely chopped
- 1 lb/450 g ground lamb
- 2 tbsp tomato paste
- 2 tbsp all-purpose flour
- 1¼ cups chicken stock
- 1 tsp ground cinnamon
- 4 oz/115 g dried macaroni
- 2 beefsteak tomatoes, sliced
- 1¼ cups strained plain yogurt
- 2 eggs, lightly beaten
- salt and pepper

1 Preheat the oven to 375°F/190°C.

2 Heat the oil in a large, heavy-bottom skillet. Add the onion and garlic and cook over low heat, stirring occasionally, for 5 minutes, or until softened. Add the lamb and cook, breaking it up with a wooden spoon, until browned all over.

3 Add the tomato paste and sprinkle in the flour. Cook, stirring, for 1 minute, then stir in the stock. Season to taste with salt and pepper and stir in the cinnamon. Bring to a boil, reduce the heat, cover, and cook for 25 minutes.

4 Meanwhile, bring a large, heavy-bottom pan of lightly salted water to a boil. Add the pasta, return to a boil, and cook for 8–10 minutes, or until tender but still firm to the bite.

5 Drain the pasta and stir into the lamb mixture. Spoon into a large, ovenproof dish and arrange the tomato slices on top. Beat together the yogurt and eggs, then spoon over the lamb mixture. Bake in the preheated oven for 1 hour, or until the topping is golden brown. Serve immediately.

lamb & potato moussaka

serves 4
- 1 large eggplant, sliced
- 1 tbsp olive oil
- 1 onion, finely chopped
- 1 garlic clove, crushed
- 12 oz/350 g lean ground lamb
- 2¾ cups sliced mushrooms
- 15 oz/425 g canned chopped tomatoes with herbs
- ⅔ cup lamb stock
- 2 tbsp cornstarch
- 2 tbsp water
- 1 lb 2 oz/500 g potatoes, parboiled for 10 minutes and sliced
- 2 eggs
- generous ½ cup soft cheese
- ⅔ cup plain yogurt
- ½ cup grated sharp cheddar cheese
- salt and pepper

1 Preheat the oven to 375°F/190°C.

2 Lay the eggplant slices on a clean board and sprinkle with salt. Let stand for 10 minutes, then turn the slices over and repeat. Place in a colander, rinse, and drain.

3 Meanwhile, heat the oil in a large pan. Add the onion and garlic and cook for 3–4 minutes. Add the lamb and mushrooms and cook over medium heat for 5 minutes, or until browned. Stir in the tomatoes and stock, bring to a boil, and simmer for 10 minutes. Mix the cornstarch and water together to make a smooth paste, then stir into the pan. Cook, stirring constantly, until thickened.

4 Spoon half the mixture into an ovenproof dish. Cover with the eggplant slices, then the remaining lamb mixture. Arrange the sliced potatoes on top.

5 Beat the eggs, soft cheese, and yogurt together. Season to taste with salt and pepper, then pour over the potatoes to cover. Sprinkle over the cheese and bake in the preheated oven for 45 minutes, or until the topping is golden brown. Serve immediately.

pork stroganoff

serves 4

- 12 oz/350 g lean pork tenderloin
- 1 tbsp vegetable oil
- 1 onion, chopped
- 2 garlic cloves, crushed
- 2 tbsp all-purpose flour
- 2 tbsp tomato paste
- generous 1¾ cups chicken or vegetable stock
- 1⅓ cups sliced mushrooms
- 1 large green bell pepper, seeded
- ½ tsp freshly grated nutmeg, plus extra to garnish
- 4 tbsp plain yogurt, plus extra to serve
- salt and pepper
- cooked rice, to serve
- chopped fresh parsley, to garnish

1 Trim away any excess fat or gristle from the pork, then cut the meat into ½-inch/1-cm thick slices. Heat the oil in a large, heavy-bottom skillet and gently cook the pork, onion, and garlic for 4–5 minutes, or until lightly browned.

2 Stir in the flour and tomato paste, then pour in the stock and stir to mix thoroughly. Add the mushrooms, bell pepper, nutmeg, and salt and pepper to taste. Bring to a boil, cover, and let simmer for 20 minutes, or until the pork is tender and cooked through.

3 Remove the skillet from the heat and stir in the yogurt. Transfer to warmed serving plates. Serve immediately with rice and an extra spoonful of yogurt and garnish with parsley and nutmeg.

Mmmm...

pork & vegetable stew

serves 4

- 1 lb/450 g lean boneless pork
- 1½ tbsp all-purpose flour
- 1 tsp ground coriander
- 1 tsp ground cumin
- 1½ tsp ground cinnamon
- 1 tbsp olive oil
- 1 onion, chopped
- 14 oz/400 g canned chopped tomatoes
- 2 tbsp tomato paste
- 2 cups chicken stock
- 1⅔ cups chopped carrots
- 12 oz/350 g squash, such as kabocha, peeled, seeded, and chopped
- 2½ cups sliced leeks
- ¾ cup sliced okra
- salt and pepper
- fresh parsley sprigs, to garnish
- cooked couscous, to serve

1 Trim off any fat or gristle from the pork and cut into thin strips about 2 inches/5 cm long. Mix the flour and spices together. Toss the pork in the spiced flour until well coated and reserve any remaining spiced flour.

2 Heat the oil in a large, heavy-bottom pan and cook the onion, stirring frequently, for 5 minutes, or until softened. Add the pork and cook over high heat, stirring frequently, for 5 minutes, or until browned on all sides and sealed. Sprinkle in the reserved spiced flour and cook, stirring constantly, for 2 minutes, then remove from the heat.

3 Gradually add the tomatoes to the pan. Blend the tomato paste with a little of the stock in a pitcher and gradually stir into the pan, then stir in half the remaining stock.

4 Add the carrots, then return to the heat and bring to a boil, stirring. Reduce the heat, then cover and simmer, stirring occasionally, for 1½ hours. Add the squash and cook for an additional 15 minutes.

5 Add the leeks, okra, and the remaining stock if you prefer a thinner stew. Simmer for an additional 15 minutes, or until the pork and vegetables are tender. Season to taste with salt and pepper, then garnish with parsley and serve immediately with couscous.

pork and white wine stew

serves 6

- ²⁄₃ cup all-purpose flour
- 3 lb/1.3 kg pork tenderloin, cut into ¼-inch/5-mm slices
- 4 tbsp corn oil
- 2 onions, thinly sliced
- 2 garlic cloves, finely chopped
- 14 oz/400 g canned chopped tomatoes
- 1½ cups dry white wine
- 1 tbsp torn fresh basil leaves
- 2 tbsp chopped fresh parsley
- salt and pepper
- fresh oregano sprigs, to garnish
- fresh crusty bread, to serve

1 Spread the flour on a plate and season with salt and pepper. Coat the pork slices in the flour, shaking off any excess. Heat the oil in a flameproof casserole. Add the pork slices and cook over medium heat, turning occasionally, for 4–5 minutes, or until browned all over. Transfer the pork to a plate with a slotted spoon.

2 Add the onions to the casserole and cook over low heat, stirring occasionally, for 10 minutes, or until golden brown. Add the garlic and cook for an additional 2 minutes, then add the tomatoes, wine, and basil, and season to taste with salt and pepper. Cook, stirring frequently, for 3 minutes.

3 Return the pork to the casserole, cover, and simmer gently for 1 hour, or until the meat is tender. Add the parsley, garnish with oregano sprigs, and serve immediately with fresh crusty bread.

classic french cassoulet

serves 8

- 1 lb 2 oz/500 g dried navy beans, soaked overnight
- bouquet garni
- 1 celery stalk, coarsely chopped
- 3 onions, 1 quartered, 2 thinly sliced
- 4 large garlic cloves, 2 whole, 2 chopped
- 8 cups water
- 1 lb 2 oz/500 g slab bacon, skinned
- 2 tbsp duck fat or vegetable oil
- 14 oz/400 g Toulouse or pork sausage
- 14 oz/400 g lamb shoulder, boned and cut into 4 large chunks
- 2 tbsp tomato paste
- 1¼ cups fresh breadcrumbs
- salad greens, to serve

1 Drain and rinse the beans and put them in a large saucepan with the bouquet garni, celery, onion quarters, and whole garlic cloves. Add the water and bring to a boil. Skim off any foam, then reduce the heat to low. Gently simmer for 1 hour, uncovered.

2 Meanwhile, cut the slab bacon into 1½-inch/4-cm pieces, then add the duck fat to a large, heavy-bottom saucepan and place over a high heat. Add the slab bacon and cook until browned all over. Remove and reserve, then repeat with the sausages, then the lamb. Add the sliced onions, chopped garlic, and tomato paste and cook in the remaining fat for 2 minutes. Remove from the heat and let cool.

3 Preheat the oven to 350°F/180°C.

4 Drain the beans, reserving the liquid but discarding the vegetables. In a large casserole, layer the beans and meat alternately until they're all used up. Add the onion mixture and enough of the bean-cooking liquid to almost cover. Sprinkle over the breadcrumbs, cover, and cook in the preheated oven for 1 hour. Reduce the heat to 275°F/140°C, uncover, and cook for an additional hour.

5 Make sure that the cassoulet isn't too dry, adding a little heated bean liquid or water if necessary. Serve immediately with salad greens.

catalan pork stew

serves 4–6
- 2 tbsp olive oil
- 4 lb 8 oz/2 kg boneless pork shoulder, cut into 3-inch/7.5-cm chunks
- bouquet garni
- 3 cups white wine
- 3–4 carrots, cut into ½-inch/1-cm slices
- 1 lb 2 oz/800 g canned chickpeas, drained and rinsed
- salt and pepper

sofregit
- 2 onions, chopped
- ½ cup olive oil
- 4 large tomatoes, grated, skins and cores discarded
- 4 large garlic cloves, finely chopped
- 1 tbsp hot Spanish paprika

picada
- 1 slice day-old country bread, fried in olive oil
- 1 tbsp blanched almonds, toasted
- 1 tbsp skinned hazelnuts, toasted
- 2 garlic cloves, crushed
- 1 oz/30 g bittersweet chocolate
- olive oil, as required

1 For the sofregit, put the onions and oil in a large pan and place over medium–high heat. Cook, stirring occasionally, for 10 minutes. Reduce the heat to low and cook for an additional 10–20 minutes, until golden brown. Add the tomatoes, garlic, and paprika, and simmer, stirring, for 15 minutes.

2 Preheat the oven to 350°F/160°C. Pour the oil into a flameproof casserole and heat over medium–high heat. Brown the pork on all sides, in batches, adding more oil if necessary. Pour off any excess fat. Stir in the sofregit, bouquet garni, and salt and pepper to taste. Pour in the wine and enough water to cover, then bring to a boil. Cover and bake in the preheated oven for 1¼ hours. Stir in the carrots, re-cover the casserole, and return to the oven for 30 minutes, or until the pork and carrots are tender.

3 Meanwhile, to make the picada, tear the bread into a food processor, then add the almonds, hazelnuts, garlic, and chocolate, and process until finely blended. With the motor running, slowly pour in enough oil to form a thick paste.

4 Transfer the casserole to the stove. Remove the pork and carrots with a slotted spoon and set aside. Bring the cooking liquid to a boil and place several ladlefuls in a heatproof bowl. Stir in the picada until well blended, then stir this mixture into the casserole, and boil for 2 minutes. Reduce the heat and add the pork, carrots, and chickpeas. Simmer for about 5 minutes, or until the stew thickens. Serve immediately.

pot-roast pork

serves 4

- 1 tbsp sunflower oil
- 4 tbsp butter
- 2 lb 4 oz/1 kg boned and rolled pork loin joint
- 4 shallots, chopped
- 6 juniper berries
- 2 fresh thyme sprigs, plus extra to garnish
- ⅔ cup hard cider
- ⅔ cup chicken stock or water
- 8 celery stalks, chopped
- 2 tbsp all-purpose flour
- ⅔ cup heavy cream
- salt and pepper

1 Heat the oil with half the butter in a large, heavy-bottom saucepan or flameproof casserole. Add the pork and cook over medium heat, turning frequently, for 5–10 minutes, or until browned. Transfer to a plate.

2 Add the shallots to the pan and cook, stirring frequently, for 5 minutes, or until softened. Add the juniper berries and thyme sprigs and return the pork to the pan with any juices that have collected on the plate. Pour in the cider and stock, season to taste with salt and pepper, then cover and simmer for 30 minutes. Turn the pork over and add the celery. Re-cover the pan and cook for an additional 40 minutes.

3 Meanwhile, make a beurre manié by mashing the remaining butter with the flour in a small bowl. Transfer the pork and celery to a platter with a slotted spoon and keep warm. Remove and discard the juniper berries and thyme. Whisk the beurre manié, a little at a time, into the simmering cooking liquid. Cook, stirring constantly, for 2 minutes, then stir in the cream and bring to a boil.

4 Slice the pork and spoon a little of the sauce over it. Garnish with the thyme sprigs and serve immediately. Hand around the remaining sauce separately.

ham stew with black-eyed peas

serves 4

- 1–1 lb 4 oz/450–550 g lean ham
- 2½ tbsp olive oil
- 1 onion, chopped
- 2–3 garlic cloves, chopped
- 2 celery stalks, chopped
- scant 1½ cups carrots, sliced
- 1 cinnamon stick, bruised
- ½ tsp ground cloves
- ¼ tsp freshly grated nutmeg
- 1 tsp dried oregano
- scant 2 cups chicken stock or vegetable stock
- 1–2 tbsp maple syrup
- 3 large spicy sausages, about 8 oz/225 g, casings removed
- 14 oz/400 g canned black-eyed peas or fava beans, drained and rinsed
- 1 orange bell pepper, seeded and chopped
- 1 tbsp cornstarch
- 2 tbsp water
- pepper

1 Trim off any fat or skin from the ham and cut into 1½-inch/4-cm chunks. Heat 1 tablespoon of the oil in a heavy-bottom pan and cook the ham over high heat, stirring frequently, for 5 minutes, or until browned on all sides. Using a slotted spoon, remove from the pan and set aside.

2 Add the onion, garlic, celery, and carrots to the pan with 1 tablespoon of the remaining oil and cook over medium heat, stirring frequently, for 5 minutes, or until softened. Add all the spices, season to taste with salt and pepper, and cook, stirring constantly, for 2 minutes.

3 Return the ham to the pan. Add the oregano, stock, and maple syrup to taste, then bring to a boil, stirring. Reduce the heat, then cover and simmer, stirring occasionally, for 1 hour.

4 Heat the remaining oil in a skillet and cook the spicy sausages, turning frequently, until browned all over. Remove and cut each into 3–4 chunks, then add to the pan. Add the black-eyed peas and bell pepper and simmer for an additional 20 minutes. Blend the cornstarch with the water and stir into the stew, then cook for 3–5 minutes. Serve immediately.

pork, sausage & rice casserole

serves 4

- 2 tbsp corn oil
- 2 tbsp butter
- 1 lb/450 g pork tenderloin, cut into thin strips
- 1 large onion, chopped
- 1 red bell pepper, seeded and sliced
- 1 orange bell pepper, seeded and sliced
- 2 cups sliced mushrooms
- ¾ cup long-grain rice
- generous 1¾ cups beef stock
- 8 oz/225 g smoked sausage, sliced
- ¼ tsp ground allspice
- salt and pepper
- 2 tbsp chopped fresh parsley, to garnish

1 Preheat the oven to 350°F/180°C.

2 Heat the oil and butter in a large, flameproof casserole. Add the pork and cook over medium heat, stirring, for 5 minutes, until browned. Transfer to a plate.

3 Add the onion and cook over low heat, stirring occasionally, for 5 minutes, or until softened. Stir in the bell peppers and cook, stirring frequently, for an additional 4–5 minutes. Add the mushrooms and cook for 1 minute, then stir in the rice. Cook for 1 minute, or until the grains are well coated, then add the stock and bring to a boil.

4 Return the pork to the casserole, add the sausage and allspice, and season to taste with salt and pepper. Mix thoroughly, cover, and cook in the preheated oven for 1 hour, or until all the liquid has been absorbed and the meat is tender. Serve immediately, garnished with chopped parsley.

pork & pasta casserole

serves 4

- 2 tbsp olive oil
- 1 onion, chopped
- 1 garlic clove, finely chopped
- 2 carrots, diced
- 2 oz/55 g pancetta, chopped
- 1½ cups chopped mushrooms
- 1 lb/450 g ground pork
- ½ cup dry white wine
- 4 tbsp strained tomatoes
- 7 oz/200 g canned chopped tomatoes
- 2 tsp chopped fresh sage, plus extra sprigs to garnish
- 8 oz/225 g dried penne pasta
- 5 oz/140 g mozzarella cheese, diced
- 4 tbsp freshly grated Parmesan cheese
- 1¼ cups Béchamel Sauce (see page 9)
- salt and pepper

1 Preheat the oven to 400°F/200°C.

2 Heat the oil in a large, heavy-bottom skillet. Add the onion, garlic, and carrots and cook over low heat, stirring occasionally, for 5 minutes, or until the onion has softened. Add the pancetta and cook for 5 minutes. Add the mushrooms and cook, stirring occasionally, for an additional 2 minutes. Add the pork and cook, breaking it up with a wooden spoon, until the meat is browned all over. Stir in the wine, the strained and chopped tomatoes, and the chopped sage. Season to taste with salt and pepper, bring to a boil, then cover and simmer over low heat for 25–30 minutes.

3 Meanwhile, bring a large, heavy-bottom pan of lightly salted water to a boil. Add the pasta, return to a boil, and cook for 8–10 minutes, or until tender but still firm to the bite.

4 Spoon the pork mixture into a large, ovenproof dish. Stir the mozzarella and half the Parmesan into the Béchamel Sauce. Drain the pasta and stir the sauce into it, then spoon it over the pork mixture. Sprinkle with the remaining Parmesan and bake in the preheated oven for 25–30 minutes, or until golden brown. Serve immediately, garnished with sage sprigs.

Mmmm...
poultry

coq au vin

serves 4

- 2 tbsp butter
- 8 pearl onions
- 4½ oz/125 g lean bacon, coarsely chopped
- 4 fresh chicken joints
- 1 garlic clove, finely chopped
- 12 button mushrooms
- 1¼ cups red wine
- bouquet garni
- 1 tbsp chopped fresh tarragon
- 2 tsp cornstarch
- 1–2 tbsp cold water
- salt and pepper
- chopped fresh flat-leaf parsley, to garnish

1 Melt half of the butter in a large skillet over medium heat. Add the onions and bacon and cook, stirring, for 3 minutes. Lift out the bacon and onions with a slotted spoon and set aside.

2 Melt the remaining butter in the skillet and add the chicken. Cook for 3 minutes, then turn over and cook on the other side for 2 minutes. Drain off any excess chicken fat. Return the bacon and onions to the skillet, then add the garlic, mushrooms, wine, bouquet garni, and tarragon. Season to taste with salt and pepper. Cook for about 1 hour, or until the juices run clear when a skewer is inserted into the thickest part of the meat.

3 Remove from the heat, lift out the chicken, onions, bacon, and mushrooms with a slotted spoon, and transfer them to a serving platter, and keep warm. Discard the bouquet garni.

4 Mix the cornstarch with the water, then stir it into the juices in the skillet. Bring to a boil, lower the heat, and cook, stirring, for 1 minute. Pour the sauce over the chicken and serve, garnished with parsley.

chicken casserole with dumplings

serves 4

- 4 chicken quarters
- 2 tbsp sunflower oil
- 2 leeks, trimmed and sliced
- 1 cup chopped carrots
- 2 cups chopped parsnips
- 2 small turnips, chopped
- 2½ cups chicken stock
- 3 tbsp Worcestershire sauce
- 2 fresh rosemary sprigs
- salt and pepper

dumplings

- 1¾ cups self-rising flour
- scant ½ cup lard or vegetable shortening
- 1 tbsp chopped rosemary leaves
- salt and pepper

1 Remove the skin from the chicken if you prefer. Heat the oil in a large, flameproof casserole or heavy-bottom pan and sauté the chicken until golden. Using a slotted spoon, remove the chicken from the pan. Drain off the excess fat.

2 Add the leeks, carrots, parsnips, and turnips to the casserole and cook for 5 minutes, until lightly colored. Return the chicken to the pan. Add the stock, Worcestershire sauce, rosemary sprigs, and salt and pepper to taste, then bring to a boil. Reduce the heat, cover, and simmer gently for about 50 minutes, or until the juices run clear when the chicken is pierced with a skewer.

3 To make the dumplings, combine the flour, lard, and chopped rosemary with salt and pepper to taste in a bowl. Stir in just enough water to bind to a firm dough.

4 Form into 8 small balls and place on top of the chicken and vegetables. Cover and simmer for an additional 10–12 minutes, until the dumplings are well risen. Serve immediately.

chicken, tomato & onion casserole

serves 4

- 1½ tbsp unsalted butter
- 2 tbsp olive oil
- 4 lb/1.8 kg skinned chicken portions, bone in
- 2 red onions, sliced
- 2 garlic cloves, finely chopped
- 14 oz/400 g canned chopped tomatoes
- 2 tbsp chopped fresh flat-leaf parsley
- 6 fresh basil leaves, torn
- 1 tbsp sun-dried tornato paste
- ⅔ cup red wine
- 2½ cups sliced mushrooms
- salt and pepper

1 Preheat the oven to 325°F/160°C.

2 Melt the butter with the oil in a flameproof casserole. Add the chicken and cook, turning frequently, for 5–10 minutes, until golden brown all over. Transfer to a plate, using a slotted spoon.

3 Add the onions and garlic to the casserole and cook over low heat, stirring occasionally, for 10 minutes, until golden. Add the tomatoes, parsley, basil, sun-dried tomato paste, and wine, and season to taste with salt and pepper. Bring to a boil, then return the chicken pieces to the casserole, pushing them down into the sauce.

4 Cover and cook in the preheated oven for 50 minutes. Add the mushrooms and cook for an additional 10 minutes, or until the chicken pieces are tender and the juices run clear when a skewer is inserted into the thickest part of the meat. Serve immediately.

chicken with 40 garlic cloves

serves 4

- 3 lb 4 oz–4 lb 8 oz/ 1.5–2 kg chicken
- ½ lemon
- 40 whole garlic cloves, peeled
- 2 tbsp olive oil
- 4 fresh thyme sprigs
- 2 fresh rosemary sprigs
- 4 fresh parsley sprigs
- 1 large carrot, coarsely chopped
- 2 celery stalks, coarsely chopped
- 1 onion, coarsely chopped
- generous 1½ cups white wine
- salt and pepper
- crusty French bread and salad greens, to serve

1 Preheat the oven to 400°F/200°C.

2 Stuff the chicken with the ½ lemon and 4 of the garlic cloves. Rub the chicken with a little of the oil and some salt and pepper.

3 In a large, flameproof casserole, spread out the remaining garlic cloves, the herbs, carrot, celery, and onion, then place the chicken on top. Pour over the remaining oil and add the wine. Cover with a tight-fitting lid, place in the preheated oven, and cook for 1¼ hours.

4 Remove the chicken from the casserole and check that it's cooked by inserting a skewer into the thickest part of the meat; the juices should run clear. Cover and keep warm. Remove the garlic cloves and reserve.

5 Place the casserole over low heat and simmer the juices for 5 minutes to make a gravy. Strain, reserving the vegetables.

6 Carve the chicken and serve it with the vegetables from the casserole. Squeeze the flesh out of the garlic cloves and spread it on the bread. Serve immediately, accompanied by salad greens.

chicken & barley stew

serves 4

- 2 tbsp vegetable oil
- 8 small, skinless chicken thighs
- generous 2 cups chicken stock
- scant ½ cup pearl barley, rinsed and drained
- 7 small new potatoes, scrubbed and cut in half lengthwise
- 2 large carrots, sliced
- 1 leek, sliced
- 2 shallots, sliced
- 1 tbsp tomato paste
- 1 bay leaf
- 1 zucchini, sliced
- 2 tbsp chopped fresh flat-leaf parsley, plus extra sprigs to garnish
- 2 tbsp all-purpose flour
- 4 tbsp water
- salt and pepper

1 Heat the oil in a large saucepan over medium heat. Add the chicken and cook for 3 minutes, then turn over and cook on the other side for 2 minutes. Add the stock, barley, potatoes, carrots, leek, shallots, tomato paste, and bay leaf. Bring to a boil, lower the heat, and simmer for 30 minutes.

2 Add the zucchini and chopped parsley, cover the pan, and cook for 20 minutes, or until the chicken is cooked through and the juices run clear when a skewer is inserted into the thickest part of the meat. Remove the bay leaf and discard.

3 In a separate bowl, mix the flour with the water and stir into a smooth paste. Add it to the stew and cook, stirring, over low heat, for an additional 5 minutes. Season to taste with salt and pepper.

4 Remove from the heat, ladle into individual serving bowls, and garnish with parsley sprigs. Serve immediately.

Mmmm...

chicken & pumpkin casserole

serves 4

- 3 tbsp olive oil
- 5 lb/2.25 kg chicken, cut into 8 pieces and dusted with flour
- 7 oz/200 g spicy sausage, thickly sliced
- small bunch of fresh sage leaves
- 1 onion, chopped
- 6 garlic cloves, sliced
- 2 celery stalks, sliced
- 1 small pumpkin or butternut squash, peeled, seeded, and coarsely chopped
- 1 cup dry sherry
- 2½ cups chicken stock
- 14 oz/400 g canned chopped tomatoes
- 2 bay leaves
- small bunch of fresh flat-leaf parsley, chopped
- salt and pepper

1 Preheat the oven to 350°F/180°C.

2 Heat the oil in a casserole and fry the chicken with the spicy sausage and sage leaves, until golden brown. Remove with a slotted spoon and reserve.

3 Add the onion, garlic, celery, and pumpkin and cook for 20 minutes, or until the mixture is golden brown.

4 Add the sherry, stock, tomatoes, and bay leaves, and season to taste with salt and pepper. Return the reserved chicken, spicy sausage, and sage to the casserole, cover, and cook in the preheated oven for 1 hour.

5 Remove from the oven, stir in the parsley, and serve immediately.

chicken & butternut squash casserole

serves 4

- 2 tbsp olive oil
- 4 skinless, boneless chicken thighs, about 3½ oz/100 g each, cut into bite-size pieces
- 1 large onion, sliced
- 2 leeks, chopped
- 2 garlic cloves, chopped
- 1 butternut squash, peeled, seeded, and cut into cubes
- 2 carrots, diced
- 14 oz/400 g canned chopped tomatoes with herbs
- 14 oz/400 g canned mixed beans, drained and rinsed
- scant ½ cup vegetable or chicken stock, plus extra if needed
- salt and pepper

1 Preheat the oven to 325°F/160°C.

2 Heat half the oil in a large, flameproof casserole over high heat, then add the chicken and cook, turning frequently, for 2–3 minutes, or until browned all over. Reduce the heat to medium, then remove the chicken with a slotted spoon and set aside.

3 Add the remaining oil to the casserole, then add the onion and leeks and cook, stirring occasionally, for 10 minutes, or until softened. Add the garlic, squash, and carrots, and cook, stirring, for 2 minutes. Add the tomatoes, beans, and stock, then stir well and bring to a simmer.

4 Cover, then transfer to the preheated oven and cook for 1–1¼ hours, stirring once or twice—if the casserole looks too dry, add a little extra stock. Season to taste with salt and pepper. Serve immediately.

garlic chicken casserole

serves 4

- 4 tbsp sunflower oil
- 2 lb/900 g skinless, boneless chicken breast, chopped
- 3 cups sliced mushrooms
- 16 shallots
- 6 garlic cloves, finely chopped
- 1 tbsp all-purpose flour
- 1 cup white wine
- 1 cup chicken stock
- bouquet garni
- 1 celery stalk
- 14 oz/400 g canned borlotti beans, drained and rinsed
- salt and pepper
- steamed squash and crusty bread, to serve

1 Preheat the oven to 300°F/150°C.

2 Heat the oil in a flameproof casserole and sauté the chicken until browned all over. Remove the chicken from the casserole with a slotted spoon and set aside until required.

3 Add the mushrooms, shallots, and garlic to the casserole and cook for 4 minutes. Return the chicken to the casserole and sprinkle with the flour, then cook for an additional 2 minutes.

4 Add the wine and stock, stir until boiling, then add the bouquet garni and celery. Season to taste with salt and pepper. Add the beans.

5 Cover and cook in the preheated oven for 2 hours. Remove the bouquet garni and celery stalk and serve the casserole immediately with squash and bread.

chicken in riesling

serves 4–6

- 2 tbsp all-purpose flour
- 1 chicken, weighing
  3 lb 8 oz/1.6 kg, cut into
  8 pieces, or 8 chicken thighs
- 4 tbsp unsalted butter
- 1 tbsp sunflower oil
- 4 shallots, finely chopped
- 12 mushrooms, sliced
- 2 tbsp brandy
- generous 2 cups
  Riesling wine
- generous 1 cup
  heavy cream
- salt and pepper
- chopped fresh flat-leaf
  parsley, to serve

1 Season the flour with salt and pepper to taste and toss the chicken pieces in it to coat. Shake off any excess.

2 Melt half the butter with the oil in a large flameproof casserole over medium–high heat. Add the chicken pieces, in batches, and cook, turning frequently, until browned all over. Remove from the casserole and set aside.

3 Pour off all the fat and wipe the casserole clean with paper towels. Melt the remaining butter in the casserole, add the shallots and mushrooms, and sauté, stirring constantly, for 3 minutes. Return the chicken to the casserole and remove from the heat.

4 Warm the brandy in a small saucepan, ignite, and pour it over the chicken pieces to flambé. When the flames die down, return to the heat, pour in the wine, and bring to a boil. Reduce the heat, cover, and simmer for 40–45 minutes, until the chicken is tender and the juices run clear when a skewer is inserted into the thickest part of the meat. Transfer the chicken to a serving platter and keep warm.

5 Skim the fat from the surface of the cooking liquid. Stir in the cream, then bring to a boil and reduce by half. Season to taste with salt and pepper. Spoon the sauce over the chicken pieces and sprinkle with parsley. Serve immediately.

chicken biryani

serves 8

- 1½ tsp finely chopped fresh ginger
- 1½ tsp crushed garlic
- 1 tbsp garam masala
- 1 tsp chili powder
- 2 tsp salt
- 1¼ cups plain yogurt
- 5 crushed cardamom pods
- 3 lb 5 oz/1.5 kg chicken
- ⅔ cup milk
- 1 tsp saffron strands
- 6 tbsp ghee
- 2 onions, sliced
- 1 lb/450 g basmati rice
- 2 cinnamon sticks
- 4 fresh green chiles
- 4 tbsp lemon juice
- 2 tbsp cilantro leaves

1 Mix the ginger, garlic, garam masala, chili powder, half the salt, the yogurt, and the cardamom pods in a bowl. Skin and cut the chicken into 8 pieces, add to the spices, and mix well. Cover and let marinate in the refrigerator for 3 hours.

2 Boil the milk in a small saucepan, pour over the saffron, and set aside.

3 Heat the ghee in a saucepan. Add the onions and cook until golden. Transfer half of the onions and ghee to a bowl and set aside.

4 Place the rice and cinnamon sticks in a saucepan of water. Bring the rice to a boil and remove from the heat when half-cooked. Drain and place in a bowl. Mix with the remaining salt.

5 Chop the chiles and set aside. Add the chicken mixture to the pan containing the onions. Add half of the chiles, lemon juice, cilantro, and saffron milk. Add the rice, then the rest of the ingredients, including the reserved onions and ghee. Cover tightly. Cook over low heat for 1 hour, or until the juices run clear when a skewer is inserted into the thickest part of the meat.

Mmmm...

chicken with apricots & chickpeas

serves 4

- 2 tbsp olive or sunflower oil
- 1 large chicken, cut into 8 pieces, or 8 chicken thighs
- 2 large onions, sliced
- 2 large garlic cloves, crushed
- 2 tsp ground coriander
- 1½ tsp ground ginger
- 1½ tsp ground cumin
- pinch of dried chile flakes, to taste (optional)
- 2½ cups dried apricots, soaked in 1¼ cups orange juice
- 14 oz/400 g canned chickpeas, drained and rinsed
- large pinch of saffron threads
- 1 preserved lemon, rinsed and sliced
- ¼ cup slivered almonds, toasted
- fresh flat-leaf parsley sprigs, to garnish
- cooked couscous, to serve

1 Heat the oil in a flameproof casserole over medium–high heat. Add as many chicken pieces as will fit without overcrowding and sauté for 3–5 minutes, until golden brown. Remove from the casserole and set aside while you sauté the remaining pieces.

2 Pour off all but 2 tablespoons of the oil from the casserole. Add the onions and stir for 4 minutes. Add the garlic and continue stirring for 1–2 minutes, until the onions are softened but not browned. Stir in the coriander, ginger, cumin, and chile flakes, if using, and cook, stirring, for 1 minute.

3 Return the chicken pieces to the casserole with enough water to cover. Bring to a boil, then reduce the heat and let simmer for 20 minutes. Add the apricots, chickpeas, and saffron and continue to simmer for 10 minutes, or until the chicken pieces are cooked through and the juices run clear when a skewer is inserted into the thickest part of the meat.

4 Transfer the chicken, apricots, and chickpeas to a serving platter and keep warm. Bring the liquid in the casserole to a boil and reduce by half. Pour this liquid over the chicken, add the preserved lemon, and sprinkle with the slivered almonds. Transfer to serving plates, garnish with parsley sprigs, and serve immediately with couscous.

chicken with apples

serves 4
- 1 tbsp olive oil
- 4 chicken portions, about 5½ oz/150 g each, skinned if preferred
- 1 onion, chopped
- 2 celery stalks, coarsely chopped
- 1½ tbsp all-purpose flour
- 1¼ cups clear apple juice
- ⅔ cup chicken stock
- 1 baking apple, cored and cut into quarters
- 2 bay leaves
- 1–2 tsp honey
- 1 yellow bell pepper, seeded and cut into chunks
- 1 large or 2 medium apples, cored and sliced
- 1 tbsp butter, melted
- 2 tbsp raw brown sugar
- salt and pepper
- 1 tbsp chopped fresh mint, to garnish

1 Preheat the oven to 375°F/190°C.

2 Heat the oil in a deep skillet and cook the chicken over medium–high heat, turning frequently, for 10 minutes, or until golden all over and sealed. Using a slotted spoon, transfer to a casserole.

3 Add the onion and celery to the skillet and cook over medium heat, stirring frequently, for 5 minutes, or until softened. Sprinkle in the flour and cook, stirring constantly, for 2 minutes, then remove from the heat. Gradually stir in the apple juice and stock, then return to the heat and bring to a boil, stirring. Add the baking apple, bay leaves, and honey. Season to taste with salt and pepper.

4 Pour over the chicken in the casserole, then cover and cook in the preheated oven for 25 minutes. Add the bell pepper and cook for an additional 10–15 minutes, or until the chicken is tender and the juices run clear when a skewer is inserted into the thickest part of the meat.

5 Meanwhile, preheat the broiler to high. Brush the apple slices with half the butter, then sprinkle with half the sugar and cook under the broiler for 2–3 minutes, or until the sugar has caramelized. Turn the slices over, brush with the remaining butter, sprinkle with the remaining sugar, and cook for an additional 2 minutes. Serve the casserole immediately, garnished with the apple slices and mint.

one-pot chicken & rice

serves 4

- 2 tbsp butter
- 1 tbsp sunflower oil
- 4 large chicken breasts, skin removed
- 1 onion, chopped
- 1 garlic clove, crushed
- 2 red or green bell peppers, halved, seeded, and finely chopped
- ⅓ cup corn kernels
- generous ⅓ cup peas
- 1 bay leaf, torn in half
- scant 1 cup dry white wine
- ⅔ cup quick-cooking brown rice
- generous 1 cup chicken stock
- salt and pepper
- chopped fresh parsley, to garnish

1 Melt the butter with the oil in a large, flameproof casserole over medium–high heat. Add as many chicken breasts as will fit without overcrowding the casserole and fry, turning occasionally for 3–5 minutes, until golden brown on all sides. Remove from the casserole and cook the remaining chicken breasts, then remove those from the casserole.

2 Pour off all but 1 tablespoon of the oil from the casserole. Add the onion, garlic, and bell peppers and cook, stirring, for about 5 minutes, until softened but not browned. Return the chicken pieces to the casserole, add the corn, peas, and bay leaf, then add the wine and simmer until it is almost all evaporated.

3 Scatter the rice over the chicken pieces, making sure it rests on top of the chicken, then pour in the stock and enough water to cover all the chicken pieces. Season to taste with salt and pepper.

4 Bring to a boil, cover, and reduce the heat to low. Let the chicken and rice cook for 20 minutes, until all the liquid has been absorbed, the rice is tender, and the juices run clear when a skewer is inserted into the thickest part of the meat.

5 Taste and adjust the seasoning, adding salt and pepper if needed. Scatter over the parsley and serve immediately.

chicken casserole with a herb crust

serves 4

- 2 tbsp all-purpose flour
- 4 whole chicken legs
- 1 tbsp olive oil
- 1 tbsp butter
- 1 onion, chopped
- 3 garlic cloves, sliced
- 4 parsnips, peeled and cut into large chunks
- 1 cup dry white wine
- 3½ cups chicken stock
- 3 leeks, white parts only, sliced
- ⅔ cup prunes, halved (optional)
- 1 tbsp English mustard
- bouquet garni
- 2 cups fresh breadcrumbs
- ⅔ cup crumbled feta cheese
- ½ cup mixed chopped tarragon and flat-leaf parsley
- salt and pepper

1 Preheat the oven to 350°F/180°C.

2 Season the flour with salt and pepper to taste and toss the chicken in it to coat. Shake off any excess.

3 Heat the oil and butter in a flameproof casserole over medium heat. Add the chicken and cook, turning frequently, until browned all over. Remove with a slotted spoon and keep warm.

4 Add the onion, garlic, and parsnips to the casserole and cook for 20 minutes, or until the mixture is golden brown.

5 Add the wine, stock, leeks, prunes (if using), mustard, and bouquet garni. Season to taste with salt and pepper. Return the chicken to the casserole, cover, and cook in the preheated oven for 1 hour, or until the juices run clear when a skewer is inserted into the thickest part of the meat. Meanwhile, mix together the breadcrumbs, cheese, and herbs.

6 Remove the casserole from the oven and increase the temperature to 400°F/200°C. Uncover the casserole and sprinkle over the breadcrumb mixture. Return to the oven for 10 minutes, uncovered, until the crust starts to brown. Serve immediately.

chicken cobbler

serves 4

- 2 tbsp all-purpose flour
- 4 skinless, boneless chicken breasts, cut into bite-size chunks
- 2 tbsp butter
- 2 tbsp olive oil
- 1 large leek, sliced
- 2 scallions, chopped
- 1 garlic clove, crushed
- 2 carrots, chopped
- 1 orange bell pepper, seeded and chopped
- 1 tbsp tomato paste
- ½ tsp ground turmeric
- ¾ cup white wine
- ¾ cup chicken stock
- 1 bay leaf
- salt and pepper

cobbler topping

- 1¼ cups self-rising flour, plus extra for dusting
- 2 tsp baking powder
- ½ tsp ground turmeric
- pinch of salt
- 3 tbsp butter
- 4–5 tbsp milk

1 Preheat the oven to 350°F/180°C. Put the flour in a bowl with salt and pepper to taste. Add the chicken and toss in the flour to coat. Reserve any remaining flour.

2 Melt the butter with the oil in a large, flameproof casserole, add the chicken, and cook, stirring, until the chicken is browned all over. Lift out with a slotted spoon, transfer to a plate, and set aside.

3 Add the leek, scallions, and garlic to the casserole and cook over medium heat, stirring, for 2 minutes, until softened. Add the carrots and bell pepper and cook for 2 minutes, then stir in the remaining seasoned flour, the tomato paste, and turmeric. Pour in the wine and stock, bring to a boil, then reduce the heat and cook over low heat, stirring, until thickened. Return the chicken to the pan, add the bay leaf, cover, then bake in the preheated oven for 30 minutes.

4 Meanwhile, sift the flour, baking powder, turmeric, and salt into a mixing bowl. Rub in the butter until the mixture resembles fine breadcrumbs, then stir in enough of the milk to make a smooth dough. Transfer to a lightly floured board, knead lightly, then roll out to a thickness of about ½ inch/1 cm. Cut out circles using a 2-inch/5-cm cookie cutter.

5 Remove the casserole from the oven and discard the bay leaf. Arrange the dough circles over the top, then return to the oven and bake for an additional 30 minutes, or until the cobbler topping has risen and is lightly golden.

potato, leek & chicken pie

serves 4

- 8 oz/225 g waxy potatoes, diced
- 7½ tbsp butter
- 1 skinless, boneless chicken breast, about 6 oz/175 g, diced
- 1 leek, sliced
- 1⅔ cups sliced cremini mushrooms
- 2½ tbsp all-purpose flour
- 1¼ cups milk
- 1 tbsp Dijon mustard
- 2 tbsp chopped fresh sage
- 8 oz/225 g filo pastry, thawed if frozen
- salt and pepper

1 Preheat the oven to 350°F/180°C. Cook the potatoes in a pan of boiling water for 5 minutes. Drain and set aside.

2 Melt 5 tablespoons of the butter in a skillet and cook the chicken for 5 minutes, or until browned all over.

3 Add the leek and mushrooms and cook over medium heat, stirring occasionally, for 3 minutes. Stir in the flour and cook, stirring constantly, for 1 minute. Gradually add the milk and bring to a boil. Add the mustard, sage, and potatoes, and simmer for 10 minutes.

4 Meanwhile, melt the remaining butter in a small saucepan. Line a deep pie plate with half of the sheets of filo pastry. Spoon the chicken mixture onto the plate and cover with 1 sheet of pastry. Brush the pastry with a little of the melted butter and lay another sheet on top. Brush this sheet with butter.

5 Cut the remaining filo pastry into strips and fold them onto the top of the pie to create a ruffled effect. Brush the strips with the remaining melted butter and cook in the preheated oven for 45 minutes, or until golden brown and crisp. Serve immediately.

mexican turkey

serves 4

- 6 tbsp all-purpose flour
- 4 turkey breast fillets
- 3 tbsp corn oil
- 1 onion, thinly sliced
- 1 red bell pepper, seeded and sliced
- 1¼ cups chicken stock
- 2 tbsp raisins
- 4 tomatoes, peeled, seeded, and chopped
- 1 tsp chili powder
- ½ tsp ground cinnamon
- pinch of ground cumin
- 1 oz/25 g semisweet chocolate, finely chopped or grated
- salt and pepper
- fresh cilantro sprigs, to garnish

1 Preheat the oven to 325°F/160°C.

2 Spread the flour on a plate and season well with salt and pepper. Coat the turkey fillets in the seasoned flour, shaking off any excess. Reserve any remaining seasoned flour.

3 Heat the oil in a flameproof casserole. Add the turkey fillets and cook over medium heat, turning occasionally, for 5–10 minutes, or until browned all over. Transfer to a plate with a slotted spoon.

4 Add the onion and bell pepper to the casserole. Cook over low heat, stirring occasionally, for 5 minutes, or until softened. Sprinkle in any remaining seasoned flour and cook, stirring constantly, for 1 minute. Gradually stir in the stock, then add the raisins, tomatoes, chili powder, cinnamon, cumin, and chocolate. Season to taste with salt and pepper. Bring to a boil, stirring constantly.

5 Return the turkey to the casserole, cover, and cook in the preheated oven for 50 minutes, until cooked through and the juices run clear when a skewer is inserted into the thickest part of the meat. Serve immediately, garnished with cilantro sprigs.

turkey in a piquant sauce

serves 4

- 2 tbsp all-purpose flour
- 2 lb 4 oz/1 kg turkey pieces
- 2 tbsp butter
- 1 tbsp corn oil
- 2 onions, sliced
- 1 garlic clove, finely chopped
- 1 red bell pepper, seeded and sliced
- 14 oz/400 g canned chopped tomatoes
- bouquet garni
- ⅔ cup chicken stock
- salt and pepper
- 2 tbsp chopped fresh parsley, to garnish

1 Spread the flour on a plate and season well with salt and pepper. Coat the turkey in the seasoned flour, shaking off any excess. Reserve any remaining seasoned flour.

2 Melt the butter with the oil in a flameproof casserole or large pan. Add the turkey and cook over medium heat, stirring, for 5–10 minutes, or until browned all over. Transfer the turkey to a plate with a slotted spoon and keep warm.

3 Add the onions, garlic, and bell pepper to the casserole and cook, stirring occasionally, for 5 minutes, or until softened. Sprinkle in the reserved seasoned flour and cook, stirring constantly, for 1 minute.

4 Return the turkey to the casserole, then add the tomatoes, bouquet garni, and stock. Bring to a boil, stirring constantly, then cover and simmer for 1¼ hours, or until the turkey is cooked through and tender.

5 Transfer the turkey to a serving platter with a slotted spoon. Discard the bouquet garni. Return the sauce to a boil and cook until reduced and thickened. Season to taste with salt and pepper and pour over the turkey. Serve immediately, garnished with parsley.

turkey with mole

serves 4

- 4 turkey portions, each cut into 4 pieces
- about 2 cups chicken stock, plus extra for thinning
- about 1 cup water
- 1 onion, chopped
- 1 whole garlic bulb, divided into cloves and peeled
- 1 celery stalk, chopped
- 1 bay leaf
- 1 bunch fresh cilantro, finely chopped
- 2¼ cups mole sauce (use prepared mole paste, thinned as per the package directions)
- 4–5 tbsp sesame seeds, to garnish

1 Preheat the oven to 375°F/190°C.

2 Arrange the turkey in a large, flameproof casserole. Pour the stock and water around the turkey, then add the onion, garlic, celery, bay leaf, and half the cilantro. Cover and bake in the preheated oven for 1–1½ hours, or until the turkey is tender. Add extra liquid if needed.

3 Warm the mole sauce in a pan with enough stock to make it the consistency of thin cream.

4 Place the sesame seeds in a dry skillet and dry-roast, shaking the skillet, until lightly golden.

5 Arrange the turkey pieces on a serving plate and spoon the warmed mole sauce over the top. Sprinkle with the sesame seeds and the remaining cilantro. Serve immediately.

italian turkey steaks

serves 4

- 1 tbsp olive oil
- 4 turkey scallops or steaks
- 2 red bell peppers, seeded and sliced
- 1 red onion, sliced
- 2 garlic cloves, finely chopped
- 1¼ cups strained tomatoes
- ⅔ cup medium white wine
- 1 tbsp chopped fresh marjoram
- 14 oz/400 g canned cannellini beans, drained and rinsed
- 3 tbsp fresh white breadcrumbs
- salt and pepper
- fresh basil sprigs, to garnish

1 Heat the oil in a flameproof casserole. Add the turkey scallops and cook over medium heat for 5–10 minutes, turning occasionally, until browned all over. Transfer to a plate using a slotted spoon.

2 Add the bell peppers and onion to the casserole and cook over low heat, stirring occasionally, for 5 minutes, or until softened. Add the garlic and cook for an additional 2 minutes.

3 Return the turkey to the casserole and add the strained tomatoes, wine, and marjoram. Season to taste with salt and pepper. Bring to a boil, then reduce the heat, cover, and simmer, stirring occasionally, for 25–30 minutes, or until the turkey is cooked through and tender. Meanwhile, preheat the broiler to medium.

4 Stir in the cannellini beans. Simmer for an additional 5 minutes. Sprinkle the breadcrumbs over the top and place under the preheated broiler for 2–3 minutes, or until golden. Serve immediately, garnished with basil sprigs.

duck in spiced orange sauce

serves 6

- 1 tbsp vegetable oil
- 6 duck legs 6–8 oz/ 175–225 g each
- 2 lemongrass stalks
- 8 large garlic cloves, crushed
- 1½-inch/4-cm piece fresh ginger, thinly sliced
- 6 scallions, 4 crushed, 2 thinly sliced diagonally
- 4 cups freshly squeezed orange juice
- freshly squeezed juice of 2 limes
- ¼ cup fish sauce
- 1 tbsp granulated sugar
- 1 tsp five-spice powder
- 6 star anise
- 4 fresh red Thai chiles or dried red Chinese (tien sien) chiles
- 2–3 cups water
- salt and pepper
- cooked rice and lime wedges, to serve

1 Heat the oil in a large saucepan over high heat, then add the duck legs and cook for 20 minutes, cooking the first side until crisp and coming off the bottom of the pan easily, then turning over and cooking the other side.

2 Meanwhile, discard the bruised leaves and root ends of the lemongrass stalks, then halve and crush 6–8 inches/15–20 cm of the lower stalks.

3 Transfer the duck legs to a plate using a slotted spoon. Drain off most of the fat from the saucepan, leaving about 1 tablespoon in the pan. Heat over high heat, then add the garlic, ginger, and crushed scallions and stir-fry for 5 minutes, or until fragrant and golden. Add the orange juice, lime juice, fish sauce, sugar, five-spice powder, lemongrass, star anise, and chiles.

4 Reduce the heat to low–medium and return the duck legs to the saucepan. Add enough of the water to cover by about 1 inch/2.5 cm. Simmer, partially covered, for 3–4 hours, or until the meat is tender and falling off the bones.

5 Adjust the seasoning, adding salt and pepper if needed. Remove the fat that has risen to the surface with a spoon. Garnish with the sliced scallions and serve immediately with rice and lime wedges.

duck legs with olives

serves 4

- 4 duck legs, all visible fat removed
- 1 lb 12 oz/800 g canned chopped tomatoes
- 8 garlic cloves, peeled but left whole
- 1 large onion, chopped
- 1 carrot, finely chopped
- 1 celery stalk, finely chopped
- 3 fresh thyme sprigs
- generous ½ cup Spanish green olives in brine, stuffed with pimientos, garlic, or almonds, drained and rinsed
- 1 tsp finely grated orange rind
- salt and pepper

1 Put the duck legs in a flameproof casserole or a large, heavy-bottom skillet with a tight-fitting lid. Add the tomatoes, garlic, onion, carrot, celery, thyme, and olives, and stir together. Season to taste with salt and pepper.

2 Turn the heat to high and cook, uncovered, until the ingredients start to bubble. Reduce the heat to low, cover tightly, and let simmer for 1¼–1½ hours, until the duck is tender. Check occasionally and add a little water if the mixture appears to be drying out.

3 When the duck is tender, transfer it to a serving platter with a slotted spoon, cover, and keep warm. Increase the heat to medium, and cook, uncovered, for about 10 minutes, until the mixture forms a sauce. Stir in the orange rind, then adjust the seasoning, adding salt and pepper if needed.

4 Mash the tender garlic cloves with a fork and spread over the duck legs. Spoon the sauce over the top. Serve immediately.

duck & red wine casserole

serves 4

- 4 duck portions, about 5½ oz/150 g each, all visible fat removed
- 2 tbsp olive oil
- 1 red onion, cut into wedges
- 2–3 garlic cloves, chopped
- 1 large carrot, chopped
- 2 celery stalks, chopped
- 2 tbsp all-purpose flour
- 1¼ cups red wine, such as claret
- 2 tbsp brandy (optional)
- ⅔–generous ¾ cup chicken stock or water
- 3-inch/7.5-cm strip of orange zest
- 2 tsp red currant jelly
- 1¼ cups snow peas
- generous 1¾ cups button mushrooms
- salt and pepper
- 1 tbsp chopped fresh parsley, to garnish

1 Heat a large, deep skillet for 1 minute, until warm but not piping hot. Put the duck portions in the skillet and heat gently until the fat starts to run. Increase the heat a little, then cook, turning over halfway through, for 5 minutes, or until browned on both sides. Transfer to a flameproof casserole.

2 Add 1 tablespoon of the oil to the skillet and cook the onion, garlic, carrot, and celery, stirring frequently, for 5 minutes, or until softened. Sprinkle in the flour and cook, stirring constantly, for 2 minutes, then remove the skillet from the heat.

3 Gradually stir in the wine, brandy (if using), and stock, then return to the heat and bring to a boil, stirring. Season to taste with salt and pepper, then add the orange zest and red currant jelly. Pour over the duck portions in the casserole, then cover and simmer, stirring occasionally, for 1–1¼ hours.

4 Cook the snow peas in a pan of boiling water for 3 minutes, then drain and add to the stew. Meanwhile, heat the remaining oil in a small pan and cook the mushrooms, stirring frequently, for 3 minutes, or until beginning to soften. Add to the casserole. Cook the casserole for an additional 5 minutes, or until the duck is tender. Serve immediately, garnished with the parsley.

duck jambalaya-style stew

serves 4

- 4 duck breasts, about 5½ oz/150 g each
- 2 tbsp olive oil
- 8 oz/225 g piece ham, cut into small chunks
- 8 oz/225 g spicy sausage, outer casing removed
- 1 onion, chopped
- 3 garlic cloves, chopped
- 3 celery stalks, chopped
- 1–2 fresh red chiles, seeded and chopped
- 1 green bell pepper, seeded and chopped
- 2½ cups chicken stock
- 1 tbsp chopped fresh oregano
- 14 oz/400 g canned chopped tomatoes
- 1–2 tsp hot pepper sauce, or to taste
- fresh parsley sprigs, to garnish
- salad greens and cooked rice, to serve

1 Remove and discard the skin and any fat from the duck breasts. Cut the flesh into bite-size pieces.

2 Heat half the oil in a large, deep skillet and cook the duck, ham, and spicy sausage over high heat, stirring frequently, for 5 minutes, or until browned on all sides. Using a slotted spoon, remove from the skillet and set aside.

3 Add the onion, garlic, celery, and chile to the skillet and cook over medium heat, stirring frequently, for 5 minutes, or until softened. Add the bell pepper, then stir in the stock, oregano, tomatoes, and hot pepper sauce.

4 Bring to a boil, then reduce the heat and return the duck, ham, and spicy sausage to the skillet. Cover and simmer, stirring occasionally, for 20 minutes, or until the duck and ham are tender.

5 Serve immediately, garnished with parsley sprigs and accompanied by salad greens and rice.

braised asian duck

serves 4

- 3 tbsp soy sauce
- ½ tsp five-spice powder
- 4 duck legs or breasts, cut into pieces
- 3 tbsp vegetable oil
- 1 tsp sesame oil
- 1 tsp finely chopped fresh ginger
- 1 large garlic clove, finely chopped
- 4 scallions, white part thickly sliced, green part shredded
- 2 tbsp rice wine or dry sherry
- 1 tbsp oyster sauce
- 3 star anise
- 2 tsp black peppercorns
- 2–2½ cups chicken stock or water
- 8 oz/225 g canned water chestnuts, drained
- 2 tbsp cornstarch
- salt and pepper

1 Combine 1 tablespoon of the soy sauce, the five-spice powder, and salt and pepper to taste and rub over the duck pieces. Heat 2½ tablespoons of the vegetable oil in a flameproof casserole, add the duck, and cook, turning occasionally, until browned all over. Transfer to a plate with a slotted spoon.

2 Drain the fat from the casserole and wipe out with paper towels. Heat the sesame oil and the remaining vegetable oil. Add the ginger and garlic. Cook for a few seconds. Add the sliced white scallions and cook for a few seconds.

3 Return the duck to the casserole. Add the rice wine, oyster sauce, star anise, peppercorns, and the remaining soy sauce. Pour in just enough of the stock to cover and add the water chestnuts. Bring to a boil, cover, and simmer gently for 1½ hours, adding more water if needed.

4 Mix the cornstarch with 2 tablespoons of the cooking liquid to a smooth paste. Add to the casserole, stirring until the sauce has thickened. Garnish with the shredded green scallion and serve immediately.

Mmmm...
fish &
seafood

bouillabaisse

serves 8
- 2 lb 12 oz/1.25 kg sea bass, filleted, skinned, and cut into bite-size chunks
- 2 lb 12 oz/1.25 kg red snapper, filleted, skinned, and cut into bite-size chunks
- 3 tbsp extra virgin olive oil
- grated rind of 1 orange
- 1 garlic clove, finely chopped
- pinch of saffron threads
- 2 tbsp pastis, such as Pernod
- 1 lb/450 g mussels
- 1 large cooked crab
- 1 small fennel bulb, finely chopped
- 2 celery stalks, finely chopped
- 1 onion, finely chopped
- 5 cups fish stock
- 8 small new potatoes, scrubbed
- 2 medium tomatoes, peeled, seeded, and chopped
- 1 lb/450 g large shrimp, peeled and deveined
- salt and pepper

1 Put the fish pieces in a large bowl and add 2 tablespoons of the oil, the orange rind, garlic, saffron, and pastis. Toss the fish pieces until well coated, then cover and let marinate in the refrigerator for 30 minutes.

2 Meanwhile, clean the mussels by scrubbing or scraping the shells and pulling out any beards. Discard any with broken shells and any that refuse to close when tapped. Remove the meat from the crab, chop, and reserve.

3 Heat the remaining oil in a large, flameproof casserole and cook the fennel, celery, and onion over low heat, stirring occasionally, for 5 minutes, or until softened. Add the stock and bring to a boil. Add the potatoes and tomatoes, and cook over medium heat for 7 minutes.

4 Reduce the heat and add the fish to the stew, beginning with the thickest pieces, then add the mussels, shrimp, and crab and simmer until the fish is opaque, the mussels have opened, and the shrimp have turned pink. Discard any mussels that remain closed. Season to taste with salt and pepper and serve immediately.

seafood chili

serves 4

- 4 oz/115 g shrimp, peeled and deveined
- 9 oz/250 g prepared scallops, thawed if frozen
- 4 oz/115 g monkfish fillet, cut into pieces
- 1 lime, peeled and thinly sliced
- 1 tbsp chili powder
- 1 tsp ground cumin
- 2–3 tbsp chopped fresh cilantro
- 2 garlic cloves, finely chopped
- 1 fresh green chile, seeded and chopped
- 3 tbsp corn oil
- 1 onion, coarsely chopped
- 1 red bell pepper, seeded and coarsely chopped
- 1 yellow bell pepper, seeded and coarsely chopped
- ¼ tsp ground cloves
- pinch of ground cinnamon
- pinch of cayenne pepper
- 1½ cups fish stock
- 14 oz/400 g canned chopped tomatoes
- 14 oz/400 g canned red kidney beans, drained and rinsed
- salt

1 Place the shrimp, scallops, monkfish, and lime slices in a large, nonmetallic dish with ¼ teaspoon of the chili powder, ¼ teaspoon of the cumin, 1 tablespoon of the cilantro, half the garlic, the chile, and 1 tablespoon of the oil. Cover with plastic wrap and let marinate for up to 1 hour.

2 Meanwhile, heat 1 tablespoon of the remaining oil in a flameproof casserole or large, heavy-bottom pan. Add the onion, the remaining garlic, and the bell peppers and cook over low heat, stirring occasionally, for 5 minutes, or until softened. Add the remaining chili powder, the remaining cumin, the cloves, cinnamon, and cayenne with the remaining oil, if necessary, and season to taste with salt. Cook, stirring, for 5 minutes, then gradually stir in the stock and tomatoes. Partially cover and simmer for 25 minutes.

3 Add the beans to the casserole and spoon the fish and shellfish on top. Cover and cook for 10 minutes, or until the fish and shellfish are cooked through. Sprinkle with the remaining cilantro and serve immediately.

fisherman's stew

serves 6

- 3 lb 5 oz/1.5 kg mussels
- 3 tbsp olive oil
- 2 onions, chopped
- 3 garlic cloves, finely chopped
- 1 red bell pepper, seeded and sliced
- 3 carrots, chopped
- 1 lb 12 oz/800 g canned chopped tomatoes
- ½ cup dry white wine
- 2 tbsp tomato paste
- 1 tbsp chopped fresh dill
- 2 tbsp chopped fresh parsley
- 1 tbsp chopped fresh thyme
- 1 tbsp fresh basil leaves, plus extra to garnish
- 2 lb/900 g whitefish fillets, cut into chunks
- 1 lb/450 g shrimp, peeled and deveined
- 1½ cups fish stock or water
- salt and pepper

1 Clean the mussels by scrubbing or scraping the shells and pulling off any beards. Discard any with broken shells and any that refuse to close when tapped. Rinse the mussels under cold running water.

2 Heat the oil in a flameproof casserole. Add the onions, garlic, bell pepper, and carrots, and cook over low heat, stirring occasionally, for 5 minutes, or until softened.

3 Add the tomatoes, wine, tomato paste, and herbs. Bring to a boil, then reduce the heat and simmer for 20 minutes.

4 Add the fish, mussels, shrimp, and stock, and season to taste with salt and pepper. Return the stew to a boil and simmer for 6–8 minutes, or until the shrimp have turned pink and the mussels have opened. Discard any mussels that remain closed.

5 Serve immediately, garnished with basil leaves.

mediterranean fish casserole

serves 6

- 2 tbsp olive oil
- 1 red onion, sliced
- 2 garlic cloves, chopped
- 2 red bell peppers, seeded and thinly sliced
- 14 oz/400 g canned chopped tomatoes
- 1 tsp chopped fresh oregano or marjoram
- a few saffron strands, soaked in 1 tbsp warm water for 2 minutes
- 1 lb/450 g whitefish fillets, cut into chunks
- 1 lb/450 g prepared squid, cut into rings
- 1¼ cups fish or vegetable stock
- 4 oz/115 g cooked, peeled shrimp, plus extra in their shells to garnish
- salt and pepper
- 2 tbsp chopped fresh parsley, to garnish
- crusty bread, to serve

1 Heat the oil in a skillet and fry the onion and garlic over medium heat for 2–3 minutes, until beginning to soften.

2 Add the bell peppers to the skillet and continue to cook over low heat for an additional 5 minutes. Add the tomatoes, oregano, and saffron, and stir well.

3 Preheat the oven to 400°F/200°C.

4 Place the fish in a large casserole with the squid. Pour in the vegetable mixture and the stock, stir well, and season to taste with salt and pepper.

5 Cover and cook in the preheated oven for about 30 minutes, until the fish is tender and cooked through. Add the shrimp and heat through.

6 Spoon into warmed bowls, garnished with the whole shrimp and the parsley. Serve immediately with crusty bread to mop up the casserole juices.

spanish fish in tomato sauce

serves 4

- 4 tbsp lemon juice
- 6 tbsp olive oil
- 4 swordfish steaks,
  about 6 oz/175 g each
- 1 onion, finely chopped
- 1 garlic clove,
  finely chopped
- 1 tbsp all-purpose flour
- 8 oz/225 g tomatoes,
  peeled, seeded,
  and chopped
- 1 tbsp tomato paste
- 1¼ cups dry white wine
- salt and pepper
- fresh dill sprigs, to garnish

1 Preheat the oven to 350°F/180°C.

2 Place the lemon juice and 4 tablespoons of the oil in a shallow, nonmetallic dish, stir well, and season to taste with salt and pepper. Add the swordfish steaks, turning to coat thoroughly, then cover with plastic wrap and let marinate in the refrigerator for 1 hour.

3 Heat the remaining oil in a flameproof casserole. Add the onion and cook over low heat, stirring occasionally, for 10 minutes, or until golden. Add the garlic and cook, stirring frequently, for 2 minutes. Sprinkle in the flour and cook, stirring, for 1 minute, then add the tomatoes, tomato paste, and wine. Bring to a boil, stirring.

4 Add the fish to the casserole, pushing it down into the liquid. Cover and cook in the preheated oven for 20 minutes, or until cooked through and the flesh flakes easily. Serve immediately, garnished with dill sprigs.

monkfish ragout

serves 4–6
- 2 tbsp olive oil
- 1 small onion,
  finely chopped
- 1 red bell pepper,
  seeded and cut into
  1-inch/2.5-cm pieces
- 2 cups sliced mushrooms
- 3 garlic cloves,
  finely chopped
- 1 tbsp tomato paste
- 2 tbsp chopped fresh
  flat-leaf parsley
- ½ tsp dried oregano
- 14 oz/400 g canned
  chopped tomatoes
- ⅔ cup dry red wine
- 1 lb 4 oz/550 g monkfish,
  skinned and cubed
- 1 zucchini, sliced
- salt and pepper
- 6–8 fresh basil leaves,
  shredded, to garnish
- crusty bread, to serve

1 Heat the oil in a heavy-bottom pan or flameproof casserole over medium heat. Add the onion, bell pepper, and mushrooms and cook for 5 minutes, or until beginning to soften.

2 Stir in the garlic, tomato paste, parsley, and oregano. Cook for 1 minute, then pour in the tomatoes and wine. Season to taste with salt and pepper. Bring to a boil, then simmer gently for 10–15 minutes, or until slightly thickened.

3 Add the monkfish and zucchini. Cover and simmer for 15 minutes, or until the monkfish is cooked and the zucchini is tender but still brightly colored.

4 Garnish with the basil and serve immediately with crusty bread.

seafood stew

serves 4

- 1 yellow bell pepper, seeded and quartered
- 1 red bell pepper, seeded and quartered
- 1 orange bell pepper, seeded and quartered
- 1 lb/450 g ripe tomatoes
- 2 large, fresh green chiles, such as poblano
- 6 garlic cloves, peeled but kept whole
- 2 tsp dried oregano or dried mixed herbs
- 2 tbsp olive oil, plus extra for drizzling
- 1 large onion, finely chopped
- scant 2 cups fish, vegetable, or chicken stock
- finely grated rind and juice of 1 lime
- 2 tbsp chopped fresh cilantro, plus extra to garnish
- 1 bay leaf
- 1 lb/450 g red snapper fillets, skinned and cut into chunks
- 8 oz/225 g shrimp, peeled and deveined
- 8 oz/225 g prepared squid, cut into rings
- salt and pepper
- warmed flour tortillas, to serve

1 Preheat the oven to 400°F/200°C.

2 Put the pepper quarters, skin side up, in a roasting pan with the tomatoes, chiles, and garlic. Sprinkle with the oregano and drizzle with oil. Roast in the preheated oven for 30 minutes, or until the bell peppers are well browned and softened.

3 Remove the roasted vegetables from the oven and let stand until cool enough to handle. Peel off the skins from the bell peppers, tomatoes, and chiles, and chop the flesh. Finely chop the garlic.

4 Heat the oil in a large pan and cook the onion, stirring frequently, for 5 minutes, or until softened. Add the bell peppers, tomatoes, chiles, garlic, stock, lime rind and juice, cilantro, and bay leaf with salt and pepper to taste. Bring to a boil, then stir in the fish and seafood. Reduce the heat, then cover and simmer gently for 10 minutes, or until the fish and squid are just cooked through and the shrimp have turned pink.

5 Discard the bay leaf, then garnish with cilantro and serve immediately with flour tortillas.

paella del mar

serves 6

- 1 lb/450 g mussels
- 6 squid
- ½ cup olive oil
- 1 onion, chopped
- 2 garlic cloves, finely chopped
- 1 red bell pepper, seeded and cut into strips
- 1 green bell pepper, seeded and cut into strips
- 2 cups risotto rice
- 2 tomatoes, peeled and chopped
- 1 tbsp tomato paste
- 6 oz/175 g monkfish fillet, cut into chunks
- 6 oz/175 g red snapper fillet, cut into chunks
- 6 oz/175 g whitefish fillet, cut into chunks
- generous 2 cups fish stock
- scant ¾ cup sliced green beans
- generous ¾ cup fresh or frozen peas
- 6 canned artichoke hearts, drained
- ¼ tsp saffron threads
- 12 jumbo shrimp
- salt and pepper

1 Clean the mussels by scrubbing or scraping the shells and pulling off any beards. Discard any with broken shells and any that refuse to close when tapped. Rinse the mussels under cold running water.

2 To prepare each squid, hold the body firmly and grasp the tentacles just inside the body. Pull firmly to remove the innards. Find the transparent quill and remove. Grasp the wings on the outside of the body and pull to remove the outer skin. Trim the tentacles just below the beak and reserve. Wash the body and tentacles under running water. Slice the body into rings. Drain well on paper towels.

3 Heat the oil in a paella pan or flameproof casserole. Add the onion, garlic, and bell peppers, and cook over medium heat, stirring, for 5 minutes, or until softened. Stir in the prepared squid and cook for 2 minutes. Add the rice and cook, stirring, until transparent and coated with oil.

4 Add the tomatoes, tomato paste and fish, and cook for 3 minutes, then add the stock. Gently stir in the beans, peas, artichoke hearts, and saffron, and season to taste with salt and pepper.

5 Arrange the mussels around the edge of the pan and top the mixture with the shrimp. Bring to a boil, reduce the heat, and simmer, shaking the pan from time to time, for 15–20 minutes, or until the rice is tender. Discard any mussels that remain closed. Serve immediately.

squid stew

serves 4

- 1 lb 10 oz/750 g squid
- 3 tbsp olive oil
- 1 onion, chopped
- 3 garlic cloves, finely chopped
- 1 tsp chopped fresh thyme leaves
- 14 oz/400 g canned chopped tomatoes
- ⅔ cup red wine
- 1¼ cups water
- 1 tbsp chopped fresh parsley
- salt and pepper
- crusty bread, to serve

1 Preheat the oven to 275°F/140°C.

2 To prepare each squid, hold the body firmly and grasp the tentacles just inside the body. Pull firmly to remove the innards. Find the transparent quill and remove. Grasp the wings on the outside of the body and pull to remove the outer skin. Trim the tentacles just below the beak and reserve. Wash the body and tentacles under running water. Slice the body into rings. Drain well on paper towels.

3 Heat the oil in a large, flameproof casserole. Add the prepared squid and cook over medium heat, stirring occasionally, until lightly browned.

4 Reduce the heat and add the onion, garlic, and thyme. Cook for an additional 5 minutes, until softened.

5 Stir in the tomatoes, wine, and water. Bring to a boil, then transfer to the preheated oven and cook for 2 hours. Stir in the parsley and season to taste with salt and pepper. Serve immediately with crusty bread.

seafood in saffron sauce

serves 4

- 8 oz/225 g mussels
- 8 oz/225 g clams
- 2 tbsp olive oil
- 1 onion, sliced
- pinch of saffron threads
- 1 tbsp chopped fresh thyme
- 2 garlic cloves, finely chopped
- 1 lb 12 oz/800 g canned tomatoes, drained and chopped
- ¾ cup dry white wine
- 8 cups fish stock
- 12 oz/350 g red snapper fillets, cut into bite-size chunks
- 1 lb/450 g monkfish fillet, cut into bite-size chunks
- 8 oz/225 g prepared squid, cut into rings
- 2 tbsp fresh shredded basil leaves
- salt and pepper
- crusty bread, to serve

1 Clean the mussels and clams by scrubbing or scraping the shells and pulling out any beards that are attached to the mussels. Discard any with broken shells and any that refuse to close when tapped.

2 Heat the oil in a large, flameproof casserole and cook the onion with the saffron and thyme over low heat, stirring occasionally, for 5 minutes, or until softened. Add the garlic and cook, stirring, for 2 minutes.

3 Add the tomatoes, wine, and stock, then season to taste with salt and pepper and stir well. Bring to a boil, then reduce the heat and simmer for 15 minutes.

4 Add the fish chunks and simmer for an additional 3 minutes. Add the clams, mussels, and squid rings and simmer for an additional 5 minutes, or until the mussels and clams have opened. Discard any that remain closed. Stir in the basil and serve immediately, accompanied by crusty bread to mop up the broth.

louisiana gumbo

serves 6

- 2 tbsp sunflower-seed or corn oil
- 1¾ cups sliced okra
- 2 onions, finely chopped
- 4 celery stalks, finely chopped
- 1 garlic clove, finely chopped
- 2 tbsp all-purpose flour
- ½ tsp sugar
- 1 tsp ground cumin
- 3 cups fish stock
- 1 red bell pepper, seeded and chopped
- 1 green bell pepper, seeded and chopped
- 2 large tomatoes, chopped
- 4 tbsp chopped fresh parsley
- 1 tbsp chopped fresh cilantro
- dash of Tabasco sauce
- 12 oz/350 g whitefish fillets, skinned and cut into 2.5-cm/1-inch chunks
- 12 oz/350 g monkfish fillet skinned and cut into 2.5-cm/1-inch chunks
- 12 oz/350 g large shrimp, peeled and deveined
- salt and pepper

1 Heat half the oil in a large, flameproof casserole or large pan with tight-fitting lid and cook the okra over low heat, stirring frequently, for 5 minutes, or until browned. Using a slotted spoon, remove the okra from the casserole and set aside.

2 Heat the remaining oil in the casserole and cook the onion and celery over medium heat, stirring frequently, for 5 minutes, or until softened. Add the garlic and cook, stirring, for 1 minute. Sprinkle in the flour, sugar, and cumin with salt and pepper to taste. Cook, stirring constantly, for 2 minutes, then remove from the heat.

3 Gradually stir in the stock, then return to the heat and bring to a boil, stirring. Return the okra to the casserole and add the bell peppers and tomatoes. Partially cover, reduce the heat to low, and simmer gently, stirring occasionally, for 10 minutes.

4 Add the herbs and Tabasco sauce to taste. Gently stir in the fish and shrimp. Cover and simmer gently for 5 minutes, or until the fish is cooked through and the shrimp have turned pink. Transfer to a warmed serving dish and serve immediately.

catfish stew

serves 4

- 2 tsp garlic granules
- 1 tsp celery salt
- 1 tsp pepper
- 1 tsp curry powder
- 1 tsp paprika
- pinch of superfine sugar
- 4–8 slices catfish or rockfish, about 2 lb/900 g total weight
- 2 tbsp red wine vinegar
- 2 tbsp all-purpose flour
- 6 tbsp corn oil
- 1 onion, finely chopped
- 2 garlic cloves, finely chopped
- 2 medium tomatoes, peeled and chopped
- 1 fresh marjoram sprig
- 2½ cups fish stock
- ¼ tsp ground cumin
- ¼ tsp ground cinnamon
- 2 fresh red or green chiles, seeded and finely chopped
- 1 red bell pepper, seeded and finely chopped
- 1 yellow bell pepper, seeded and finely chopped
- salt
- fresh flat-leaf parsley sprigs, to garnish
- crusty bread, to serve

1 Mix together the garlic granules, celery salt, pepper, curry powder, paprika, and sugar in a small bowl. Place the fish in a nonmetallic dish and sprinkle with half the spice mixture. Turn the fish over and sprinkle with the remaining spice mixture. Add the vinegar and turn to coat. Cover with plastic wrap and set aside in a cool place to marinate for 1 hour.

2 Spread out the flour in a shallow dish. Drain the fish and dip into the flour to coat, shaking off any excess.

3 Heat 4 tablespoons of the oil in a skillet. Add the fish and cook over medium heat for 2–3 minutes on each side. Remove with a slotted spoon and set aside.

4 Wipe out the skillet with paper towels, add the remaining oil, and heat. Add the onion and cook over low heat, stirring occasionally, for 5 minutes, until soft. Add the garlic and cook, stirring, for an additional 2 minutes. Add the tomatoes and marjoram, increase the heat to medium, and cook, stirring occasionally, for 8 minutes.

5 Stir in the stock, cumin, and cinnamon, and add the fish, chiles, and bell peppers. Bring to a boil, then reduce the heat and simmer for 8–10 minutes, until the fish flakes easily and the sauce has thickened. Season to taste with salt. Garnish with parsley sprigs and serve immediately with crusty bread.

french fish stew

serves 4-6

- large pinch of saffron threads
- 2 tbsp olive oil
- 1 large onion, finely chopped
- 1 fennel bulb, thinly sliced, green fronds reserved
- 2 large garlic cloves, crushed
- 4 tbsp pastis
- 4 cups fish stock
- 2 large ripe tomatoes, peeled, seeded, and diced
- 1 tbsp tomato paste
- 1 bay leaf
- pinch of sugar
- pinch of dried chile flakes (optional)
- 25 large shrimp, peeled and deveined
- 1 prepared squid, cut into rings
- 2 lb/900 g Mediterranean fish fillets, such as sea bass, monkfish, or red snapper, cut into large pieces
- salt and pepper

1 Put the saffron threads in a small, dry skillet over high heat and toast, stirring constantly, for 1 minute. Immediately tip the saffron threads out of the pan and set aside.

2 Heat the oil in a large, flameproof casserole over medium heat. Add the onion and fennel, and sauté for 3 minutes, then add the garlic and continue sautéing for an additional 5 minutes, or until the onion and fennel are soft but not colored.

3 Remove the casserole from the heat. Warm the pastis in a small pan, ignite, and pour it over the onion and fennel to flambé. When the flames have died down, return the casserole to the heat and stir in the stock, tomatoes, tomato paste, bay leaf, sugar, chile flakes (if using), and salt and pepper to taste. Slowly bring to a boil, then reduce the heat to low and let simmer, uncovered, for 15 minutes.

4 Add the shrimp and squid, and simmer until the shrimp turn pink and the squid is opaque. Do not overcook. Transfer the shrimp and squid to serving bowls and keep warm.

5 Add the fish and the reserved saffron to the casserole and simmer for 5 minutes, or until the flesh flakes easily. Transfer the fish and broth to the bowls with the shrimp and squid, and garnish with the fennel fronds. Serve immediately.

moroccan fish tagine

serves 4

- 2 tbsp olive oil
- 1 large onion,
  finely chopped
- pinch of saffron threads
- ½ tsp ground cinnamon
- 1 tsp ground coriander
- ½ tsp ground cumin
- ½ tsp ground turmeric
- 7 oz/200 g canned
  chopped tomatoes
- 1¼ cups fish stock
- 4 small red snappers,
  cleaned, boned, and heads
  and tails removed
- ⅓ cup pitted green olives
- 1 tbsp chopped preserved
  lemon
- 3 tbsp chopped fresh
  cilantro
- salt and pepper

1 Heat the oil in a flameproof casserole. Add the onion and cook gently over low heat, stirring occasionally, for 10 minutes, or until softened but not colored. Add the saffron, cinnamon, coriander, cumin, and turmeric and cook for an additional 30 seconds, stirring constantly.

2 Add the tomatoes and stock and stir well. Bring to a boil, reduce the heat, cover, and simmer for 15 minutes. Uncover and simmer for 20–35 minutes, or until thickened.

3 Cut each red snapper in half, then add the fish pieces to the casserole, pushing them down into the liquid. Simmer the stew for an additional 5–6 minutes, or until the fish is just cooked.

4 Carefully stir in the olives, preserved lemon, and cilantro. Season to taste with salt and pepper and serve immediately.

seafood casserole with red wine

serves 4–6

- 12 oz/350 g mussels, scrubbed and debearded
- 4 tbsp olive oil
- 1 onion, finely chopped
- 1 green bell pepper, seeded and chopped
- 2 garlic cloves, finely chopped
- 5 tbsp tomato paste
- 1 tbsp chopped fresh flat-leaf parsley
- 1 tsp dried oregano
- 14 oz/400 g canned chopped tomatoes
- 1 cup dry red wine
- 1 lb/450 g whitefish fillets, cut into 2-inch/5-cm pieces
- 4 oz/115 g prepared scallops, halved
- 4 oz/115 g shrimp, peeled and deveined
- 7 oz/200 g canned crabmeat
- 10–15 fresh basil leaves, shredded
- salt and pepper

1 Discard any mussels with broken shells and any that refuse to close when tapped.

2 Heat the oil in a large, heavy-bottom pan or flameproof casserole over medium heat. Add the onion and bell pepper and cook for 5 minutes, or until beginning to soften.

3 Stir in the garlic, tomato paste, parsley, and oregano and cook for 1 minute, stirring.

4 Pour in the tomatoes and wine. Season to taste with salt and pepper.

5 Bring to a boil, then cover and simmer over low heat for 30 minutes. Add the fish, cover, and simmer for 15 minutes.

6 Add the mussels, scallops, shrimp, and crabmeat. Cover and cook for an additional 15 minutes. Discard any mussels that remain closed. Stir in the basil and serve immediately.

rustic fish stew

serves 4–6

- 4 tbsp olive oil
- 1 onion, chopped
- 2 celery stalks, sliced
- 3 garlic cloves, sliced
- 1 tbsp smoked paprika
- small pinch of saffron strands
- 1 cup dry sherry
- 2½ cups chicken or fish stock
- 2 bay leaves
- 14 oz/400 g canned chopped tomatoes
- 1 lb 4 oz/550 g waxy potatoes, peeled and cut into quarters
- 2 red bell peppers, seeded and sliced
- 3 lb/1.5 kg mixed seafood cut into bite-size pieces
- salt and pepper
- chopped fresh parsley and grated lemon rind, to garnish
- extra virgin olive oil, to serve

1 Heat the oil in a saucepan and fry the onion, celery, and garlic over medium heat for 2–3 minutes, until beginning to soften.

2 Add the paprika and saffron, and cook for an additional minute, then add the sherry and reduce by half.

3 Add the stock, bay leaves, tomatoes, and potatoes, season to taste with salt and pepper, and cook for 10 minutes, or until the potatoes are almost cooked. Add the bell peppers and cook for an additional 10 minutes.

4 If using mussels, clean them by scrubbing or scraping the shells and pulling off any beards. Discard any with broken shells and any that refuse to close when tapped. Rinse the mussels under cold running water.

5 Carefully add the mussels, if using, and seafood to the saucepan, stirring only once or twice. Cover and cook for 8–10 minutes, or until the seafood is cooked through. Discard any mussels that remain closed, turn off the heat, and let stand for 2 minutes.

6 Serve the stew in a large bowl, garnished with parsley and lemon rind. Drizzle with extra virgin olive oil and serve immediately.

squid with shrimp & fava beans

serves 4

- 2 tbsp olive oil
- 4 scallions, thinly sliced
- 2 garlic cloves, finely chopped
- 1 lb 2 oz/500 g prepared squid, cut into rings
- generous ⅓ cup dry white wine
- 1½ cups fresh, shelled young fava beans, 1 lb 5 oz/600 g in their pods, or 1½ cups frozen baby fava beans
- 9 oz/250 g jumbo shrimp, peeled and deveined
- 4 tbsp chopped fresh flat-leaf parsley
- salt and pepper
- crusty bread, to serve

1 Heat the oil in a large skillet with a lid or a flameproof casserole. Add the scallions and cook over medium heat, stirring occasionally, for 4–5 minutes, or until softened. Add the garlic and cook, stirring, for 30 seconds, until softened. Add the squid and cook over high heat, stirring occasionally, for 2 minutes, or until golden brown.

2 Add the wine and bring to a boil. Add the fava beans and reduce the heat, then cover and simmer for 5–8 minutes if using fresh beans, or 4–5 minutes if using frozen beans, until the beans are tender.

3 Add the shrimp and parsley, re-cover, and simmer for an additional 2–3 minutes, until the shrimp have turned pink. Season to taste with salt and pepper. Serve immediately with crusty bread to mop up the juices.

fish cobbler

serves 4
- 2 tbsp butter
- 2 large leeks, trimmed and sliced
- 1⅔ cups sliced mushrooms
- 2 zucchini, sliced
- 4 large tomatoes, peeled and chopped
- 1 tbsp chopped fresh dill
- ½ cup white wine
- ¾ cup fish stock
- 4 tsp cornstarch
- 1 lb/450 g whitefish fillets, cut into bite-size chunks
- salt and pepper

cobbler topping
- 1¼ cups self-rising flour, plus extra for dusting
- 2 tsp baking powder
- pinch of salt
- 1 tbsp chopped fresh dill
- 3 tbsp butter
- 4–5 tbsp milk

1 Preheat the oven to 400°F/200°C.

2 Melt the butter in a large, flameproof casserole over low heat. Add the leeks and cook, stirring, for 2 minutes, until slightly softened. Add the mushrooms, zucchini, tomatoes, and dill, and cook, stirring, for an additional 3 minutes.

3 Stir in the wine and stock, bring to a boil, then reduce the heat to a simmer. Mix the cornstarch with a little water to form a paste, then stir it into the casserole. Cook, stirring constantly, until thickened, then season to taste with salt and pepper and remove from the heat.

4 To make the cobbler topping, sift the flour, baking powder, and salt into a large mixing bowl. Stir in the dill, then rub in the butter with your fingertips until the mixture resembles fine breadcrumbs. Stir in enough of the milk to make a smooth dough. Transfer to a lightly floured board, knead lightly, then roll out to a thickness of about ½ inch/1 cm. Cut out circles using a 2-inch/5-cm cookie cutter.

5 Add the fish to the casserole and stir gently to mix. Arrange the dough circles over the top, then bake in the preheated oven for 30 minutes, or until the cobbler topping has risen and is lightly golden. Serve immediately.

fisherman's pie

serves 6

- 2 lb/900 g whitefish fillets, skinned
- ⅔ cup dry white wine
- 1 tbsp chopped fresh parsley, tarragon, or dill
- scant ½ cup butter, plus extra for greasing
- 3 cups sliced mushrooms
- 6 oz/175 g cooked, peeled shrimp
- 2 tbsp all-purpose flour
- ½ cup heavy cream
- 2 lb/900 g starchy potatoes, cut into chunks
- salt and pepper

1 Preheat the oven to 350°F/180°C. Grease a 7½-cup baking dish.

2 Fold the fish fillets in half and put in the prepared dish. Season well with salt and pepper, pour over the wine, and scatter over the parsley. Cover with foil and bake in the preheated oven for 15 minutes, until the fish starts to flake. Strain off the liquid and reserve for the sauce. Increase the oven temperature to 425°F/220°C.

3 Melt 1 tablespoon of the butter in a skillet over medium heat, add the mushrooms, and cook, stirring frequently, for 5 minutes. Spoon over the fish, then scatter over the shrimp.

4 Heat 4 tablespoons of the remaining butter in a pan and stir in the flour. Cook for 3–4 minutes, without browning, stirring constantly. Remove from the heat and gradually add the reserved cooking liquid, stirring well after each addition. Return to the heat and slowly bring to a boil, stirring constantly, until thickened. Add the cream and season to taste with salt and pepper. Pour over the fish in the dish and smooth over the surface.

5 Bring a large pan of lightly salted water to a boil, add the potatoes, and cook for 15–20 minutes. Drain well and mash until smooth. Season to taste with salt and pepper, then add the remaining butter, stirring until melted. Pile or pipe the potato onto the fish and sauce and bake for 10–15 minutes, until golden brown. Serve immediately.

macaroni & seafood casserole

serves 4

- 12 oz/350 g dried macaroni
- 6 tbsp butter, plus extra for greasing
- 2 small fennel bulbs, trimmed and thinly sliced
- 2 cups sliced mushrooms
- 6 oz/175 g cooked, peeled shrimp
- pinch of cayenne pepper
- 1¼ cups Béchamel Sauce (see page 9)
- ½ cup freshly grated Parmesan cheese
- 2 large tomatoes, halved and sliced
- olive oil, for brushing
- 1 tsp dried oregano
- salt

1 Preheat the oven to 350°F/180°C. Grease a large, ovenproof dish.

2 Bring a large pan of lightly salted water to a boil. Add the pasta, return to a boil, and cook for 8–10 minutes, or until tender but still firm to the bite. Drain and return to the pan. Add 2 tablespoons of the butter to the pasta, cover, shake the pan, and keep warm.

3 Melt the remaining butter in a separate pan. Add the fennel and cook for 3–4 minutes. Stir in the mushrooms and cook for an additional 2 minutes. Stir in the shrimp, then remove the pan from the heat.

4 Stir the cooked pasta, cayenne pepper, and the shrimp mixture into the Béchamel Sauce. Pour into the prepared dish and spread evenly. Sprinkle over the Parmesan and arrange the tomato slices around the edge. Brush the tomatoes with the oil, then sprinkle over the oregano. Bake in the preheated oven for 25 minutes, or until golden brown. Serve immediately.

seafood lasagna

serves 4

- 3½ tbsp butter, plus extra for greasing
- 5 tbsp all-purpose flour
- 1 tsp mustard powder
- 2½ cups milk
- 2 tbsp olive oil
- 1 onion, chopped
- 2 garlic cloves, finely chopped
- 5 cups sliced mixed mushrooms
- ⅔ cup white wine
- 14 oz/400 g canned chopped tomatoes
- 1 lb/450 g whitefish fillets, cut into chunks
- 8 oz/225 g prepared scallops
- 4–6 sheets fresh lasagna
- 8 oz/225 g mozzarella cheese, chopped
- salt and pepper

1 Preheat the oven to 400°F/200°C. Grease a rectangular, ovenproof dish.

2 Melt the butter in a pan over low heat. Add the flour and mustard powder and stir until smooth. Simmer gently for 2 minutes, then gradually add the milk, whisking until smooth. Bring to a boil, reduce the heat, and simmer for 2 minutes. Remove from the heat and reserve. Cover the surface of the sauce with plastic wrap to prevent a skin from forming.

3 Heat the oil in a skillet. Add the onion and garlic, and cook gently for 5 minutes, or until softened. Add the mushrooms and cook for 5 minutes, or until softened. Stir in the wine and boil rapidly until almost evaporated, then stir in the tomatoes. Bring to a boil, reduce the heat, and simmer, covered, for 15 minutes. Season to taste with salt and pepper and set aside.

4 Spoon half the tomato mixture over the bottom of the prepared dish, top with half the fish and scallops, and layer half the lasagna over the top. Pour over half the white sauce and sprinkle over half the mozzarella. Repeat these layers, finishing with the sauce and mozzarella.

5 Bake in the preheated oven for 35–40 minutes, or until golden and the fish is cooked through. Remove from the oven and let stand for 10 minutes before serving.

layered salmon & shrimp spaghetti

serves 6

- 12 oz/350 g dried spaghetti
- 5 tbsp butter, plus extra for greasing
- 7 oz/200 g smoked salmon, cut into strips
- 10 oz/280 g large cooked peeled shrimp
- 1¼ cups Béchamel Sauce (see page 9)
- 1 cup freshly grated Parmesan cheese
- salt
- arugula, to garnish

1 Preheat the oven to 350°F/180°C. Grease a large, ovenproof dish.

2 Bring a large pan of lightly salted water to a boil. Add the pasta, bring back to a boil, and cook for 8–10 minutes, until tender but still firm to the bite. Drain well, return to the pan, add 4 tablespoons of the butter, and toss well.

3 Spoon half the spaghetti into the prepared dish, cover with the smoked salmon, then top with the shrimp. Pour over half the Béchamel Sauce and sprinkle with half the Parmesan. Add the remaining spaghetti, cover with the remaining sauce, and sprinkle with the remaining Parmesan. Dice the remaining butter and dot it over the surface.

4 Bake in the preheated oven for 15 minutes, until the top is golden. Serve immediately, garnished with arugula.

tuna noodle casserole

serves 4–6

- 7 oz/200 g dried tagliatelle
- 2 tbsp butter
- 1 cup fresh breadcrumbs
- 14 oz/400 g canned condensed cream of mushroom soup
- ½ cup milk
- 2 celery stalks, chopped
- 1 red bell pepper, seeded and chopped
- 1 green bell pepper, seeded and chopped
- 1¼ cups coarsely grated sharp cheddar cheese
- 2 tbsp chopped fresh parsley
- 7 oz/200 g canned tuna in oil, drained and flaked
- salt and pepper

1 Preheat the oven to 400°F/200°C.

2 Bring a large pan of lightly salted water to a boil. Add the pasta, return to a boil, and cook for 2 minutes less than specified on the package directions. Drain well and set aside.

3 Meanwhile, melt the butter in a separate small pan. Stir in the breadcrumbs, then remove from the heat and set aside.

4 Pour the soup into a pan over medium heat, then stir in the milk, celery, bell peppers, half the cheese, and the parsley. Add the tuna and stir in gently. Season to taste with salt and pepper. Heat just until small bubbles appear around the edge of the mixture—do not boil.

5 Stir the pasta into the pan and use 2 forks to mix all the ingredients together. Spoon the mixture into an ovenproof dish and spread it out.

6 Stir the remaining cheese into the breadcrumb mixture, then sprinkle over the top of the pasta mixture. Bake in the preheated oven for 20–25 minutes, or until the topping is golden. Remove from the oven, then let stand for 5 minutes before serving.

Mmmm...
vegetables & beans

vegetable cassoulet

serves 8

- 3½ cups dried white beans, soaked overnight and drained
- 2 bay leaves
- 3 onions
- 4 cloves
- 1 tbsp olive oil
- 4 garlic cloves, finely chopped
- 4 leeks, sliced
- 1 lb 12 oz/800 g baby carrots
- 8 oz/225 g button mushrooms
- 1 lb 12 oz/800 g canned chopped tomatoes
- 4 tbsp chopped fresh parsley
- 1 tbsp chopped fresh savory
- 2 cups fresh breadcrumbs
- salt and pepper

1 Put the beans and bay leaves into a pan. Stud 1 of the onions with the cloves and add to the pan. Pour in enough water to cover and bring to a boil. Reduce the heat, cover, and simmer for 1 hour, then drain, reserving the cooking liquid. Remove and discard the bay leaves and onion.

2 Preheat the oven to 350°F/180°C.

3 Chop the remaining onions. Heat the oil in a flameproof casserole, then add the chopped onions, garlic, and leeks, and cook over low heat, stirring occasionally, for 5 minutes, until softened.

4 Add the carrots, mushrooms, and tomatoes, pour in 3¾ cups of the reserved cooking liquid, and season to taste with salt and pepper. Bring to a boil, then reduce the heat, cover, and simmer for 15 minutes.

5 Stir in the beans, parsley, and savory and adjust the seasoning, adding salt and pepper if needed. Sprinkle with the breadcrumbs and transfer to the preheated oven. Bake, uncovered, for 40–45 minutes, until the topping is golden brown. Serve immediately.

ratatouille

serves 8

- 1 red bell pepper, quartered
- 1 orange bell pepper, quartered
- 1 green bell pepper, quartered
- 1 lb 4 oz/550 g eggplants, thickly sliced
- 2 tbsp olive oil, plus extra for brushing
- 2 large onions, sliced
- 3 garlic cloves, finely chopped
- 1 lb/450 g zucchini, thickly sliced
- 1 lb 14 oz/850 g tomatoes, peeled, seeded, and chopped
- 1½ tsp herbes de Provence
- 2 bay leaves
- salt and pepper
- crusty bread, to serve

1 Preheat the broiler. Put the bell pepper quarters, skin side up, on a baking sheet and broil until the skins are charred and blistered. Remove with tongs, put them into a plastic bag, tie the top, and let cool. Meanwhile, spread out the eggplant slices on the baking sheet, brush with oil, and broil for 5 minutes, until lightly browned. Turn, brush with oil, and broil for an additional 5 minutes, until lightly browned. Remove with tongs.

2 Remove the bell peppers from the bag and peel off the skins. Remove and discard the seeds and membranes and cut the flesh into strips. Dice the eggplant slices.

3 Heat the oil in a large pan or flameproof casserole. Add the onions and cook over low heat, stirring occasionally, for 8–10 minutes, until lightly browned. Add the garlic and zucchini, and cook, stirring occasionally, for an additional 10 minutes.

4 Stir in the bell peppers, eggplants, tomatoes, herbes de Provence, and bay leaves. Season to taste with salt and pepper, then cover and simmer over very low heat, stirring occasionally, for 25 minutes. Remove the lid and simmer, stirring occasionally, for an additional 25–35 minutes, until all the vegetables are tender.

5 Remove and discard the bay leaves. Serve the ratatouille immediately, if serving hot, or let cool, if serving at room temperature, accompanied by crusty bread.

vegetable chili

serves 4

- 1 eggplant, cut into 1-inch/2.5-cm slices
- 1 tbsp olive oil, plus extra for brushing
- 1 large red or yellow onion, finely chopped
- 2 red or yellow bell peppers, seeded and finely chopped
- 3–4 garlic cloves, finely chopped or crushed
- 1 lb 12 oz/800 g canned chopped tomatoes
- 1 tbsp mild chili powder
- ½ tsp ground cumin
- ½ tsp dried oregano
- 2 small zucchini, cut into quarters lengthwise and sliced
- 14 oz/400 g canned kidney beans, drained and rinsed
- scant 2 cups water
- 1 tbsp tomato paste
- 6 scallions, finely chopped
- scant 1¼ cups grated cheddar cheese
- salt and pepper
- crusty bread, to serve

1 Brush the eggplant slices on one side with oil. Heat half the oil in a large, heavy-bottom skillet. Add the eggplant slices, oiled side up, and cook over medium heat for 5–6 minutes, or until browned on one side. Turn the slices over, cook on the other side until browned, and transfer to a plate. Cut into bite-size pieces and set aside.

2 Heat the remaining oil in a large pan over medium heat. Add the onion and bell peppers and cook, stirring occasionally, for 3–4 minutes, or until the onion is just softened but not browned. Add the garlic and cook for an additional 2–3 minutes, or until the onion just begins to color.

3 Add the tomatoes, chili powder, cumin, and oregano. Season to taste with salt and pepper. Bring just to a boil, reduce the heat, cover, and simmer gently for 15 minutes.

4 Add the zucchini, eggplant, and kidney beans. Stir in the water and tomato paste. Return to a boil, then cover the pan and simmer for an additional 45 minutes, or until the vegetables are tender. Taste and adjust the seasoning, adding salt and pepper if needed.

5 Ladle into warmed bowls and top with the scallions and cheese. Serve immediately with crusty bread.

tuscan bean stew

serves 4

- 1 large fennel bulb
- 2 tbsp olive oil
- 1 red onion, cut into small wedges
- 2–4 garlic cloves, sliced
- 1 fresh green chile, seeded and chopped
- 1 small eggplant, about 8 oz/225 g, cut into chunks
- 2 tbsp tomato paste
- scant 2–2½ cups vegetable stock
- 1 lb/450 g ripe tomatoes
- 1 tbsp balsamic vinegar
- a few fresh oregano sprigs
- 14 oz/400 g canned cranberry beans
- 14 oz/400 g canned flageolets
- 1 yellow bell pepper, seeded and cut into small strips
- 1 zucchini, sliced into half semicircles
- ⅓ cup pitted black olives
- ⅓ cup Parmesan cheese shavings
- salt and pepper
- crusty bread, to serve

1 Trim the fennel and reserve any feathery fronds, then cut the bulb into small strips. Heat the oil in a large, heavy-bottom pan with a tight-fitting lid and cook the onion, garlic, chile, and fennel strips, stirring frequently, for 5–8 minutes, or until softened.

2 Add the eggplant and cook, stirring frequently, for 5 minutes. Blend the tomato paste with a little of the stock in a pitcher and pour into the pan, then add the remaining stock, the tomatoes, vinegar, and oregano. Bring to a boil, then reduce the heat, cover, and simmer for 15 minutes, or until the tomatoes have begun to collapse.

3 Drain and rinse the beans, then drain again. Add them to the pan with the bell pepper, zucchini, and olives. Simmer for an additional 15 minutes, or until the vegetables are tender. Taste and adjust the seasoning, adding salt and pepper if needed. Scatter with the Parmesan shavings and serve immediately, garnished with the reserved fennel fronds and accompanied by crusty bread.

italian vegetable stew

serves 4

- 4 garlic cloves
- 1 small acorn squash, peeled and seeded
- 1 red onion, sliced
- 2 leeks, sliced
- 1 eggplant, sliced
- 1 small celery root, diced
- 2 turnips, sliced
- 2 plum tomatoes, chopped
- 1 carrot, sliced
- 1 zucchini, sliced
- 2 red bell peppers, seeded and sliced
- 1 fennel bulb, sliced
- 6 oz/175 g Swiss chard
- 2 bay leaves
- ½ tsp fennel seeds
- ½ tsp chili powder
- pinch each of dried thyme, dried oregano, and sugar
- 1 cup torn fresh basil leaves
- ½ cup extra virgin olive oil
- scant 1 cup vegetable stock
- 4 tbsp chopped fresh parsley
- salt and pepper
- 2 tbsp freshly grated Parmesan cheese, to serve

1 Finely chop the garlic and dice the squash. Put them in a large, heavy-bottom pan with all the other vegetables, the bay leaves, fennel seeds, chili powder, thyme, oregano, sugar, and half the basil. Pour in the oil and stock. Mix together well, then bring to a boil.

2 Reduce the heat, then cover and simmer for 30 minutes, or until all the vegetables are tender.

3 Sprinkle in the remaining basil and the parsley and season to taste with salt and pepper. Serve immediately, sprinkled with the cheese.

lentil bolognese

serves 4

- 1 tsp vegetable oil
- 1 tsp crushed garlic
- 2½ tbsp finely chopped onion
- ⅓ cup finely chopped leek
- ¼ cup finely chopped celery
- 3 tbsp seeded and finely chopped green bell pepper
- 3 tbsp finely chopped carrot
- ¼ cup finely chopped zucchini
- 1 cup diced Portobello mushrooms
- 4 tbsp red wine
- pinch of dried thyme
- 14 oz/400 g canned chopped tomatoes, strained through a colander, juice and pulp reserved separately
- 4 tbsp dried French lentils, cooked
- 2 tsp lemon juice
- 1 tsp sugar
- 3 tbsp chopped fresh basil, plus extra to garnish
- salt and pepper
- cooked spaghetti, to serve

1 Heat a saucepan over low heat, add the oil and garlic, and cook, stirring, until golden brown. Add all the vegetables, except the mushrooms, increase the heat to medium, and cook, stirring occasionally, for 10–12 minutes, or until softened and there is no liquid from the vegetables left in the pan.

2 Add the mushrooms. Increase the heat to high, add the wine, and cook for 2 minutes. Add the thyme and the juice from the tomatoes, and cook until reduced by half.

3 Add the lentils, stir in the tomatoes, and cook for an additional 3–4 minutes. Remove the pan from the heat and stir in the lemon juice, sugar, and basil. Season to taste with salt and pepper.

4 Serve the sauce immediately with the cooked spaghetti, garnished with basil sprigs.

vegetable & lentil casserole

serves 4

- 10 cloves
- 1 onion, peeled but kept whole
- generous 1 cup French lentils
- 1 bay leaf
- 6¼ cups vegetable stock
- 2 leeks, sliced
- 2 potatoes, diced
- 2 carrots, chopped
- 3 zucchini, sliced
- 1 celery stalk, chopped
- 1 red bell pepper, seeded and chopped
- 1 tbsp lemon juice
- salt and pepper

1 Preheat the oven to 350°F/180°C.

2 Press the cloves into the onion. Put the lentils into a large casserole, then add the onion and bay leaf and pour in the stock. Cover and cook in the preheated oven for 1 hour.

3 Remove the onion and discard the cloves. Slice the onion and return it to the casserole with the vegetables. Stir thoroughly and season to taste with salt and pepper. Cover and return to the oven for 1 hour.

4 Discard the bay leaf. Stir in the lemon juice and serve immediately, straight from the casserole.

vegetable curry

serves 4

- 1 eggplant
- 8 oz/225 g turnips
- 12 small new potatoes
- 1 small head cauliflower
- 8 oz/225 g button mushrooms
- 1 large onion
- 3 carrots
- 6 tbsp ghee
- 2 garlic cloves, crushed
- 4 tsp finely chopped fresh ginger
- 1–2 fresh green chiles, seeded and chopped
- 1 tbsp paprika
- 2 tsp ground coriander
- 1 tbsp mild or medium curry powder
- scant 2 cups vegetable stock
- 14 oz/400 g canned chopped tomatoes
- 1 green bell pepper, seeded and sliced
- 1 tbsp cornstarch
- ⅔ cup coconut milk
- 2–3 tbsp ground almonds
- salt
- fresh cilantro sprigs, to garnish
- cooked rice, to serve

1 Cut the eggplant, turnips, and potatoes into ½-inch/1-cm cubes. Divide the cauliflower into small florets. Leave the button mushrooms whole or slice thickly, if preferred. Slice the onion and carrots.

2 Heat the ghee in a large, heavy-bottom pan. Add the onion, turnips, potatoes, and cauliflower, and cook over low heat, stirring frequently, for 3 minutes. Add the garlic, ginger, chile, paprika, coriander, and curry powder and cook, stirring, for 1 minute.

3 Add the stock, tomatoes, eggplant, and mushrooms, and season to taste with salt. Cover and simmer, stirring occasionally, for 30 minutes, or until the vegetables are tender. Add the bell pepper and carrots, cover, and cook for an additional 5 minutes.

4 Place the cornstarch and coconut milk in a bowl, mix into a smooth paste, and stir into the vegetable mixture. Add the ground almonds and simmer, stirring constantly, for 2 minutes. Taste and adjust the seasoning, adding salt and pepper if needed. Transfer to warmed serving plates, garnish with cilantro sprigs, and serve immediately with rice.

spicy chickpea casserole

serves 6

- 1 tbsp cumin seeds
- 2 tbsp coriander seeds
- 2 tsp dried oregano or thyme
- 5 tbsp vegetable oil
- 2 onions, chopped
- 1 red bell pepper, seeded and cut into ¾-inch/2-cm chunks
- 1 eggplant, cut into ¾-inch/2-cm chunks
- 2 garlic cloves, chopped
- 1 fresh green chile, chopped
- 14 oz/400 g canned chopped tomatoes
- 14 oz/400 g canned chickpeas, drained and rinsed
- 8 oz/225 g green beans, cut into ¾-inch/2-cm lengths
- 2½ cups vegetable stock
- 3 tbsp chopped fresh cilantro, plus extra leaves to garnish

1 Dry-roast the seeds in a heavy-bottom skillet for a few seconds, until aromatic. Add the oregano and cook for an additional few seconds. Remove from the heat, transfer to a mortar, and crush with a pestle.

2 Heat the oil in a large, flameproof casserole. Cook the onions, bell pepper, and eggplant for 10 minutes, until softened. Add the ground seed mixture, garlic, and chile, and cook for an additional 2 minutes.

3 Add the tomatoes, chickpeas, green beans, and stock. Bring to a boil, cover, and simmer gently for 1 hour, then stir in the chopped cilantro. Serve immediately, garnished with cilantro leaves.

vegetable goulash

serves 4

- ¼ cup chopped sun-dried tomatoes (not in oil)
- generous 1 cup French lentils
- 2½ cups water
- 2 tbsp olive oil
- ½–1 tsp crushed dried chiles
- 2–3 garlic cloves, chopped
- 1 large onion, cut into small wedges
- 1 small celery root, cut into small chunks
- generous 1¾ cups sliced carrots
- 8 small new potatoes, scrubbed and cut into chunks
- 1 small acorn squash, seeded, peeled, and cut into small chunks
- 2 tbsp tomato paste
- 1¼ cups vegetable stock
- 1–2 tsp hot paprika
- a few fresh thyme sprigs, plus extra to garnish
- 1 lb/450 g ripe tomatoes
- sour cream and crusty bread, to serve

1 Put the sun-dried tomatoes in a small heatproof bowl, then cover with almost-boiling water and let soak for 15–20 minutes. Drain, reserving the soaking liquid.

2 Meanwhile, rinse and drain the lentils, then put them in a pan with the water and bring to a boil. Reduce the heat, then cover and simmer for 15 minutes. Drain and set aside.

3 Heat the oil in a large, heavy-bottom pan with a tight-fitting lid and cook the chiles, garlic, and vegetables, stirring frequently, for 5–8 minutes, or until softened. Blend the tomato paste with a little of the stock in a pitcher and pour over the vegetable mixture, then add the remaining stock, the lentils, sun-dried tomatoes and their soaking liquid, paprika, and thyme sprigs.

4 Bring to a boil, then reduce the heat and simmer for 15 minutes. Add the fresh tomatoes and simmer for an additional 15 minutes, or until the vegetables and lentils are tender. Serve immediately, topped with spoonfuls of sour cream and accompanied by crusty bread.

cold weather vegetable casserole

serves 4

- 4 tbsp butter
- 2 leeks, sliced
- 2 carrots, sliced
- 2 potatoes, cut into bite-size pieces
- 1 rutabaga, cut into bite-size pieces
- 2 zucchini, sliced
- 1 fennel bulb, halved and sliced
- 2 tbsp all-purpose flour
- 15 oz/425 g canned lima beans, drained and rinsed
- 2½ cups vegetable stock
- 2 tbsp tomato paste
- 1 tsp dried thyme
- 2 bay leaves
- salt and pepper

dumplings

- generous ¾ cup self-rising flour
- pinch of salt
- ½ cup vegetarian shortening
- 2 tbsp chopped fresh parsley
- 4 tbsp water

1 Melt the butter in large, heavy-bottom pan over low heat. Add the leeks, carrots, potatoes, rutabaga, zucchini, and fennel, and cook, stirring occasionally, for 10 minutes. Stir in the flour and cook, stirring constantly, for 1 minute. Stir in the can juices from the beans, the stock, tomato paste, thyme, and bay leaves and season to taste with salt and pepper. Bring to a boil, stirring constantly, then cover and simmer for 10 minutes.

2 To make the dumplings, sift the flour and salt into a mixing bowl, add the shortening, and mix well. Stir in the parsley and then pour in enough of the water to form a firm but soft dough. Break the dough into 8 pieces and roll them into round dumplings.

3 Add the lima beans and the dumplings to the pan, pushing them down under the liquid. Cover and let simmer for an additional 30 minutes, or until the dumplings have doubled in size.

4 Remove and discard the bay leaves and serve the stew and dumplings immediately.

lentil & rice casserole

serves 4
- 1 cup red lentils
- ⅓ cup long-grain rice
- 5 cups vegetable stock
- 1 leek, cut into chunks
- 3 garlic cloves, crushed
- 14 oz/400 g canned chopped tomatoes
- 1 tsp ground cumin
- 1 tsp chili powder
- 1 tsp garam masala
- 1 red bell pepper, seeded and sliced
- ½ cup small broccoli florets
- 8 baby corn, halved lengthwise
- ⅓ cup sliced green beans
- 1 tbsp shredded fresh basil, plus extra to garnish
- salt and pepper

1 Place the lentils, rice, and stock in a large, flameproof casserole and cook over low heat, stirring occasionally, for 20 minutes.

2 Add the leek, garlic, tomatoes, cumin, chili powder, garam masala, bell pepper, broccoli, baby corn, and green beans to the casserole.

3 Bring to a boil, reduce the heat, cover, and simmer for 10–15 minutes, or until all the vegetables are tender.

4 Add the shredded basil and season to taste with salt and pepper.

5 Garnish with basil sprigs and serve immediately.

root vegetable & pumpkin casserole

serves 4–6

- 1 onion, sliced
- 2 leeks, sliced
- 2 celery stalks, chopped
- 2 carrots, thinly sliced
- 1 red bell pepper, seeded and sliced
- 1¾ cups diced pumpkin
- 1⅔ cups diced mixed root vegetables, such as sweet potato, parsnip, and rutabaga
- 14 oz/400 g canned chopped tomatoes
- ⅔–1 cup hard cider
- 2 tsp herbes de Provence
- salt and pepper
- fresh flat-leaf parsley leaves, to garnish

1 Preheat the oven to 350°F/180°C.

2 Put the onion, leeks, celery, carrots, bell pepper, pumpkin, and root vegetables in a large casserole and mix well. Stir in the tomatoes, ⅔ cup of the hard cider, and the herbes de Provence. Season to taste with salt and pepper.

3 Cover and bake in the preheated oven, stirring once or twice, and adding a little extra cider if needed, for 1¼-1½ hours, or until the vegetables are cooked through and tender. Serve immediately, garnished with parsley leaves.

spring stew

serves 4

- ¼ cup dried cannellini beans, soaked overnight and drained
- 2 tbsp olive oil
- 4–8 pearl onions, halved
- 2 celery stalks, cut into ¼-inch/5-mm slices
- 15 baby carrots, scrubbed and halved if large
- 10 new potatoes, scrubbed and halved, or cut into quarters if large
- 3¾–5 cups vegetable stock
- bouquet garni
- 1½–2 tbsp light soy sauce
- 3 oz/85 g baby corn
- 1 cup shelled fava beans, thawed if frozen
- ½–1 head savoy or spring cabbage
- 1½ tbsp cornstarch
- 2 tbsp cold water
- salt and pepper
- ½–¾ cup grated Parmesan or sharp cheddar cheese, to serve

1 Put the beans in a large pan, add water to cover, and bring to a boil. Boil the beans rapidly for 20 minutes, then drain and set aside.

2 Heat the oil in a large, heavy-bottom pan with a tight-fitting lid, add the onions, celery, carrots, and potatoes, and cook, stirring frequently, for 5 minutes, or until softened. Add the stock, drained beans, bouquet garni, and soy sauce, then bring to a boil. Reduce the heat, cover, and simmer for 12 minutes.

3 Add the baby corn and fava beans and season to taste with salt and pepper. Simmer for an additional 3 minutes.

4 Meanwhile, discard the outer leaves and hard central core from the cabbage and shred the leaves. Add to the pan and simmer for an additional 3–5 minutes, or until all the vegetables are tender.

5 Blend the cornstarch with the water, then stir into the pan and cook, stirring, for 4–6 minutes, or until the liquid has thickened. Spoon into warmed serving bowls and sprinkle over the cheese. Serve immediately.

bean &
pasta casserole

serves 4

- 1¼ cups dried cannellini beans, soaked overnight and drained
- 8 oz/225 g dried penne pasta
- 6 tbsp olive oil
- 3½ cups vegetable stock
- 2 large onions, sliced
- 2 garlic cloves, chopped
- 2 bay leaves
- 1 tsp dried oregano
- 1 tsp dried thyme
- 5 tbsp red wine
- 2 tbsp tomato paste
- 2 celery stalks, sliced
- 1 fennel bulb, sliced
- 1¼ cups sliced mushrooms
- 1¼ cups tomatoes, sliced
- 1 tsp dark brown sugar
- scant ½ cup dry white breadcrumbs
- salt and pepper
- crusty bread, to serve

1 Preheat the oven to 350°F/180°C.

2 Put the beans in a large pan, add water to cover, and bring to a boil. Boil the beans rapidly for 20 minutes, then drain and set aside.

3 Cook the pasta in a large saucepan of boiling salted water, adding 1 tablespoon of the oil, for 3 minutes. Drain and set aside.

4 Put the beans in a large, flameproof casserole, pour in the stock, and stir in the remaining oil, the onions, garlic, bay leaves, herbs, wine, and tomato paste. Bring to a boil, cover, and cook in the preheated oven for 2 hours.

5 Remove the casserole from the oven, add the reserved pasta, the celery, fennel, mushrooms, and tomatoes, and season to taste with salt and pepper. Stir in the sugar and sprinkle the breadcrumbs on top. Cover, return to the oven, and continue cooking for 1 hour. Serve immediately with crusty bread.

mixed bean & vegetable crumble

serves 4

- 1 large onion, chopped
- 4½ oz/125 g canned red kidney beans (drained weight)
- 4½ oz/125 g canned lima beans (drained weight)
- 4½ oz/125 g canned chickpeas (drained weight)
- 2 zucchini, coarsely chopped
- 2 large carrots, coarsely chopped
- 4 tomatoes, peeled and coarsely chopped
- 2 celery stalks, chopped
- 1¼ cups vegetable stock
- 2 tbsp tomato paste
- salt and pepper

crumble topping

- 1¾ cups whole wheat breadcrumbs
- 1 tbsp finely chopped hazelnuts
- 1 tbsp chopped fresh parsley
- 1 cup grated cheddar cheese

1 Preheat the oven to 350°F/180°C.

2 Put the onion, kidney beans, lima beans, chickpeas, zucchini, carrots, tomatoes, and celery in a large, ovenproof dish. Mix together the stock and tomato paste and pour over the vegetables. Season to taste with salt and pepper. Transfer to the preheated oven and bake for 15 minutes.

3 Meanwhile, to make the crumble topping, put the breadcrumbs in a large bowl, add the hazelnuts, parsley, and cheese, and mix together well.

4 Remove the vegetables from the oven and carefully sprinkle over the crumble topping. Do not press down or it will sink into the vegetables and go mushy.

5 Return the crumble to the oven and bake for 30 minutes, or until the crumble topping is golden brown. Remove from the oven and serve immediately.

spicy vegetable cobbler

serves 4

- 1 large onion, sliced
- 2 zucchini, sliced
- 1 cup sliced mushrooms
- 2 large carrots, coarsely chopped
- 8 oz/225 g canned black-eyed peas (drained weight)
- 6 oz/175 g canned cannellini beans (drained weight)
- 14 oz/400 g canned chopped tomatoes
- 1 tsp mild chili powder
- salt and pepper

cobbler topping

- 1¼ cups self-rising flour, plus extra for dusting
- 2 tsp baking powder
- ½ tsp paprika
- pinch of salt
- 3 tbsp butter
- 4–5 tbsp milk

1 Preheat the oven to 400°F/200°C.

2 Put the onion, zucchini, mushrooms, carrots, black-eyed peas, cannellini beans, and tomatoes in a casserole. Sprinkle over the chili powder and season to taste with salt and pepper. Transfer to the preheated oven and bake for 15 minutes.

3 Meanwhile, to make the cobbler topping, sift the flour, baking powder, paprika, and salt into a large mixing bowl. Rub in the butter until the mixture resembles fine breadcrumbs, then stir in enough of the milk to make a smooth dough. Transfer to a lightly floured board, knead lightly, then roll out to a thickness of about ½ inch/1 cm. Cut out circles using a 2-inch/5-cm cookie cutter.

4 Remove the casserole from the oven, arrange the dough circles over the top, then return to the oven and bake for 30 minutes, or until the cobbler topping has risen and is lightly golden. Serve immediately.

spinach & butternut squash casserole

serves 2
- 9 oz/250 g butternut squash, seeded and cut into bite-size cubes
- 2 small red onions, each cut into 8 segments
- 2 tsp vegetable oil
- generous 4 cups baby spinach leaves
- 1 tbsp water
- 2 tbsp whole wheat breadcrumbs
- pepper

white sauce
- generous 1 cup milk
- 2 tbsp cornstarch
- 1 tsp mustard powder
- 1 small onion
- 2 bay leaves
- 4 tsp grated Parmesan or pecorino cheese

1 Preheat the oven to 400°F/200°C and warm an ovenproof serving dish.

2 Arrange the squash and red onions on a baking sheet and coat with the oil and plenty of pepper. Bake in the preheated oven for 20 minutes, turning once.

3 To make the sauce, put the milk into a small saucepan with the cornstarch, mustard powder, onion, and bay leaves. Whisk over medium heat until thick. Remove from the heat, discard the onion and bay leaves, and stir in the cheese. Set aside, stirring occasionally to prevent a skin from forming.

4 When the squash is nearly cooked, put the spinach in a large skillet with the water, stirring, for 2–3 minutes, or until just wilted.

5 Put half the squash mixture in the warmed ovenproof dish and top with half the spinach. Repeat the layers. Pour over the white sauce and sprinkle over the breadcrumbs.

6 Transfer to the oven and bake for 15–20 minutes, until the topping is golden and bubbling. Serve immediately.

baked beans with corn topping

serves 4–6

- 6 tbsp olive oil or butter
- 1 lb 10 oz/750 g onions, finely sliced
- 3–4 garlic cloves, finely chopped
- 1 tsp cumin seeds
- 1 tsp fresh or dried oregano
- 1 lb 2 oz/500 g fresh tomatoes, peeled and chopped, or canned chopped tomatoes
- 1 lb 2 oz/500 g pumpkin, peeled, seeded, and cut into small dice
- 1 lb 10 oz/750 g canned pinto or cranberry beans, drained and rinsed
- 2 tbsp chopped pitted green olives
- 2 tbsp raisins
- 1 tbsp confectioners' sugar
- 1 tsp dried chile flakes
- salt and pepper

topping

- 3 lb/1.3 kg fresh or frozen corn kernels
- generous 1½ cups milk
- 1 egg, beaten
- salt and pepper

1 Preheat the oven to 350°F/180°C.

2 Heat 4 tablespoons of the oil in a heavy-bottom pan, add the onions and garlic, and cook over low heat, stirring occasionally, for 20–30 minutes, or until softened. Add the cumin seeds, oregano, and tomatoes, and simmer for 10 minutes, or until you have a thick sauce.

3 Add the pumpkin and heat until bubbling. Reduce the heat to low, cover, and cook for an additional 10–15 minutes, or until the pumpkin is softened but not collapsed. Stir in the beans, olives, and raisins. Reheat gently and simmer for 5 minutes. Season to taste with salt and pepper.

4 Put the corn kernels in a blender or food processor with the milk and blend to a paste. Transfer to a saucepan and cook, stirring constantly, for 5 minutes, or until the mixture has thickened slightly. Remove from the heat and let cool. Stir in the egg and season to taste with salt and pepper.

5 Spread the bean mixture in an ovenproof dish and top with a thick layer of the corn mixture. Drizzle with the remaining oil and sprinkle with the sugar and chile flakes. Bake in the preheated oven for 30 minutes, or until browned and bubbling. Serve immediately.

baked eggplants

serves 4

- 3 tbsp olive oil, plus extra for oiling
- 4 eggplants
- 10½ oz/300 g mozzarella cheese, thinly sliced
- 4 slices prosciutto, shredded
- 1 tbsp chopped fresh marjoram
- 2 tbsp grated Parmesan cheese
- salt and pepper

tomato sauce

- 4 tbsp olive oil
- 1 large onion, sliced
- 4 garlic cloves, crushed
- 14 oz/400 g canned chopped tomatoes
- 1 lb/450 g fresh tomatoes, peeled and chopped
- 4 tbsp chopped fresh parsley
- 2½ cups hot vegetable stock
- 1 tbsp sugar
- 2 tbsp lemon juice
- ⅔ cup dry white wine
- salt and pepper

white sauce

- 2 tbsp butter
- 2 tbsp all-purpose flour
- 1 tsp mustard powder
- 1¼ cups milk
- freshly grated nutmeg
- salt and pepper

1 Preheat the oven to 375°F/190°C. Lightly oil a large ovenproof dish.

2 To make the tomato sauce, heat the oil in a large skillet. Add the onion and garlic, and fry until just beginning to soften. Add the canned and fresh tomatoes, parsley, stock, sugar, and lemon juice. Cover and simmer for 15 minutes. Stir in the wine and season to taste with salt and pepper.

3 Thinly slice the eggplants lengthwise. Bring a large saucepan of water to a boil and cook the eggplant slices for 5 minutes. Drain on paper towels.

4 Pour half the tomato sauce into the prepared dish with half the eggplants and drizzle with the oil. Cover with half the mozzarella, prosciutto, and marjoram. Season to taste with salt and pepper. Repeat the layers.

5 To make the white sauce, melt the butter in a large saucepan, then add the flour and mustard powder. Stir until smooth and cook over low heat for 2 minutes. Slowly beat in the milk. Simmer gently for 2 minutes. Remove from the heat, then season to taste with nutmeg, salt, and pepper.

6 Spoon the white sauce over the eggplant-and-tomato mixture, then sprinkle with the Parmesan. Bake in the preheated oven for 35–40 minutes, until the topping is golden. Serve immediately.

vegetable lasagna

serves 4

- 1 eggplant, sliced
- 3 tbsp olive oil
- 2 garlic cloves, crushed
- 1 red onion, halved and sliced
- 3 mixed bell peppers, seeded and diced
- 2½ cups sliced mixed mushrooms
- 2 celery stalks, sliced
- 1 zucchini, diced
- ½ tsp chili powder
- ½ tsp ground cumin
- 2 tomatoes, chopped
- 1¼ cups strained canned tomatoes
- 2 tbsp chopped fresh basil
- 8 no-precook lasagna verdi sheets
- salt and pepper

cheese sauce

- 2 tbsp butter or margarine
- 1 tbsp all-purpose flour
- ½ cup vegetable stock
- 1¼ cups milk
- scant ¾ cup grated cheddar cheese
- 1 tsp Dijon mustard
- 1 tbsp chopped fresh basil
- 1 egg, beaten

1 Place the eggplant slices in a colander, sprinkle with salt, and let stand for 20 minutes. Rinse under cold water, drain, and reserve.

2 Preheat the oven to 350°F/180°C.

3 Heat the oil in a saucepan. Add the garlic and onion and sauté for 1–2 minutes. Add the bell peppers, mushrooms, celery, and zucchini and cook, stirring constantly, for 3–4 minutes. Stir in the chili powder and cumin and cook for 1 minute. Mix in the tomatoes, strained canned tomatoes, and basil, and season to taste with salt and pepper.

4 For the cheese sauce, melt the butter in a saucepan. Stir in the flour and cook for 1 minute. Remove from the heat and gradually stir in the stock and milk. Return to the heat, then add half the cheese and the mustard. Boil, stirring, until thickened. Stir in the basil. Remove from the heat and stir in the egg.

5 Place half the lasagna sheets in a rectangular, ovenproof dish. Top with half the vegetable mixture and half the eggplant slices. Repeat the layers, then spoon the cheese sauce on top. Sprinkle with the remaining cheese and bake in the preheated oven for 40 minutes, or until golden. Serve immediately.

vegetable cannelloni

serves 4

- ½ cup olive oil , plus extra for greasing
- 12 dried cannelloni tubes
- 1 eggplant
- 1 cup fresh spinach
- 2 garlic cloves, crushed
- 1 tsp ground cumin
- 1¼ cups chopped mushrooms
- 2 oz/55 g mozzarella cheese, sliced
- salt and pepper
- corn salad, to garnish

tomato sauce

- 1 tbsp olive oil
- 1 onion, chopped
- 2 garlic cloves, crushed
- 1 lb 12 oz/800 g canned chopped tomatoes
- 1 tsp superfine sugar
- 2 tbsp chopped fresh basil

1 Preheat the oven to 375°F/190°C. Lightly oil a large ovenproof dish.

2 Bring a large, heavy-bottom pan of lightly salted water to a boil. Add the cannelloni tubes, return to a boil, and cook for 8–10 minutes, or until tender but still firm to the bite. Transfer the pasta to a plate and pat dry with paper towels.

3 Heat the oil in a skillet over medium heat. Add the eggplant and cook, stirring frequently, for about 2–3 minutes.

4 Add the spinach, garlic, cumin, and mushrooms and reduce the heat. Season to taste with salt and pepper and cook, stirring constantly, for 2–3 minutes. Spoon the mixture into the cannelloni tubes and arrange in the prepared dish in a single layer.

5 To make the tomato sauce, heat the oil in a pan over medium heat. Add the onion and garlic and cook for 1 minute. Add the tomatoes, sugar, and basil and bring to a boil. Reduce the heat and simmer gently for about 5 minutes. Spoon the sauce over the cannelloni tubes.

6 Arrange the mozzarella cheese on top and bake in the preheated oven for about 30 minutes, or until the cheese is golden brown and bubbling. Serve immediately, garnished with corn salad.

oven-baked risotto with mushrooms

serves 4

- 4 tbsp olive oil
- 14 oz/400 g portobello mushrooms, thickly sliced
- 4 oz/115 g pancetta or smoked bacon, diced
- 1 large onion, finely chopped
- 2 garlic cloves, finely chopped
- 1¾ cups risotto rice
- 5½ cups simmering chicken or vegetable stock
- 2 tbsp chopped fresh tarragon or flat-leaf parsley
- ¾ cup freshly grated Parmesan cheese, plus extra for sprinkling
- salt and pepper

1 Preheat the oven to 350°F/180°C.

2 Heat half the oil in a large, heavy-bottom skillet over a high heat. Add the mushrooms and stir-fry for 2–3 minutes, until golden. Transfer to a plate. Add the pancetta to the skillet and cook, stirring frequently, for 2 minutes, or until crisp and golden. Transfer to the plate with the mushrooms.

3 Heat the remaining oil in a large, flameproof casserole over medium heat. Add the onion and cook, stirring occasionally, for 2 minutes. Add the garlic and cook for 1 minute. Reduce the heat, add the rice, and mix to coat in oil. Cook, stirring constantly, for 2–3 minutes, or until the grains are translucent.

4 Gradually stir the hot stock into the rice, then add the mushroom-and-pancetta mixture and the tarragon. Season to taste with salt and pepper. Bring to a boil.

5 Cover and bake in the preheated oven for 20 minutes, or until the rice is almost tender and most of the liquid is absorbed. Uncover and stir in the Parmesan. Bake for an additional 15 minutes, until the rice is creamy. Serve immediately, sprinkled with extra Parmesan.

Index

223